Testimonies Without Boundaries

Alon Penzel
Testimonies Without Boundaries

All rights reserved
Copyright © 2024 by Alon Penzel

Published by Spines
ISBN: 979-8-89383-415-4

Testimonies Without Boundaries

Israel: October 7th 2023

Alon Penzel

Contents

"Set me as a seal upon thy heart, as a seal upon thine arm. For love is strong as death."

— The Song of Songs

Introduction

The body of testimonies in front of you documents a terrible truth, first-hand from eyewitnesses, individual stories from people's mouths, without summarizing events, without headlines and generalizations or sensationalism. We must not cover up the naked truth that was revealed before our eyes on the morning of the Black Sabbath. We must document and preserve it for generations.

Our people have fulfilled this duty throughout the generations in stories of destruction, poems, and during the Memorial Day observances of the "Shom[1]" communities. In the composition "Yeven Mezulah" (The Abyss of Despair) about the riots of 1648-1650, in Bialik's mission to document the Kishinev riots and in the dedication of Ilya Ehrenburg and Vasily Grossman to documenting in "The Black Book" the horrors of the Holocaust despite the silence and persecution of the Soviet regime.

The obligation of documentation and remembrance is, first and foremost, for our brothers and sisters to ensure that their last cry will be fully heard. Only through it can we look straight ahead and listen to the truth behind it, to its claim and fully understand the hope and prayer that it is.

An abbreviation - A common nickname for the Jewish communities in the cities of Shapira, Vermeiza and Magentza on the banks of the Rhine River. The decrees of the New Testament severely harmed these communities as a result of the Crusades.

---

1. An abbreviation - A common nickname for the Jewish communities in the cities of Shapira, Vermeiza and Magentza on the banks of the Rhine River. These communities were severely harmed by the decrees of the New Testament as a result of the Crusades.

Never back down.

The Black Sabbath was a reminder of a most difficult truth, a truth that the whole world discovered at the end of World War II and the Holocaust we went through. A truth that resulted in the oath "never again" that was fulfilled three years later with the establishment of the State of Israel and in the victory of the 1948 Independence War. The Black Sabbath was another dimension in the Jewish timeline, which illustrated to us what happens when the Jews don't have a state and what happens when the Jews don't have weapons.

But unlike the past, the oath "never again" was not a future promise. This oath took place at the same time as the Holocaust that happened to the residents of the South. On the morning of that Saturday, I saw this double revelation before my eyes when I was fighting along with my friends in the kibbutzim that surrounded Gaza. We were citizens who marched south before an order and decree, messengers of a country that did not exist. On the one hand, before our eyes, Auschwitz was resurrected, and on the other hand, before our eyes, the ghetto rebels, the partisans, the underground fighters, and the heroes of 1947-1948 also rose.

Thousands of years of destiny suddenly flowed through our veins, a Jewish destiny with an Israeli response. The ability to decide, lead, and commend even when all the forces of the universe are working against you and not to back down.

To remain human even in the face of Satan.

Do not reject a plea.

We vowed not to reject the plea because of the terror, helplessness, and evil, alongside the heroism and devotion we saw with our own eyes. Long before the first days of the war, 'ISRAEL-is' was founded to tell the personal stories of Israelis, through ordinary people, through everyday life, to bring the story of a country. October 7TH only proved this need even more. From there, we embarked on a long and arduous journey to tell the story of a nation through ordinary people, through everyday life, through those hours and through heroes, believing in the role of Israelis not only to survive and prosper but also to send a message. The belief that the global attention to what is happening in our small country is disproportionate compared to the rest of the world made us find an opportunity to proclaim the gospel that grows out of the worst of all, the gospel of the human spirit of heroism and devotion whose starting point is love and hope.

The 'ISRAEL-is' association aims to harness the potential of tens of thousands of young Israelis to tell the Israeli story in the world. Among our many actions, we joined our fellow, the author of this book, to create the document before you, a collection of testimonies without boundaries. This book demands each of us to look courageously in the face of evil, not only to commit to "never again" yet again but also not to reject a plea to bring forth the gospel of creation, growth, and hope that our existence here symbolizes.

> "Violence shall no more be heard in your land, desolation nor destruction within your borders; but you shall call your walls Salvation, and your gates Praise."

— (Isaiah 60:18)

Nimrod Palmach

CEO of ISRAEL-is

In Memory of the Victims of October 7th Terrorist Attack.

As these words are being written - children, women, elderly, and young men are still being held captive in the Gaza Strip.

This book is calling for their immediate release.

Chapter One

Testimonies from ZAKA Volunteers

F riedrich Nietzsche, a German philosopher, argued that "pain is the greatest instrument of memory." In other words, according to him, pain deeply engraves a person's memory.

According to Nietzsche, throughout human history, the perception has been established that we only remember what does not stop hurting, making the principle of "equivalent reward" necessary.

According to this principle, to guarantee the seriousness and sanctity of any promise and ensure that a debt will be repaid, the lender actually "adds" conditions to the contract and reminds the borrower that he is entitled to harm his body, his property, his family, his choices, his life and sometimes even his soul if the borrower does not keep his promise.

In the past, it was even normal to act according to a law that estimated and determined the value of body parts and organs that could be harmed according to unpaid debt.

Nietzsche believed that causing suffering, torture, blood, and sacrifices would serve as an equivalent repayment or compensation for the debt or promise that did not exist ("the pleasure in the act of violence causing suffering - a true festival").

The question arises: for what possible reason could the children of Kibbutz Be'eri be considered indebted to Hamas terrorists that they would be so brutally killed and treated as though their lives were of no value? What promise did the elderly people of Kfar Aza give to Hamas's terrorists for which they were burned alive? What debt did Hamas's terrorists try to collect from those pregnant women they never met or from those women they brutally raped?

Indeed, in this part, it is impossible to compare the events of October 7th with Nietzsche's philosophy since it is not about "equivalent reward" because there was never a debt. However, in the second part of his philosophy, Friedrich Nietzsche foresaw what was going to happen almost forty-five thousand days from the day he died. He foresaw the pleasure, the enjoyment, the satisfaction, the pride, the happiness, and the smiles, or as he called them, "a true festival" that Hamas's terrorists would experience from acts of violence and causing suffering, torture, blood, sacrifices, abuse, rape and murder, due to the slaughter they would commit.

ZAKA volunteers (in the order they are mentioned in the book):

Simcha Greinman – ZAKA volunteer for thirty-two years and the organization's international communications speaker.

Natan Kenig – ZAKA volunteer for twenty-eight years.

Moti Bukchin – The organization's speaker.

Ephraim Greidinger – ZAKA volunteer for thirty years.

Yossi Landau – ZAKA volunteer for many years.

Reuven Reuven – Responsible for vehicles and logistics in ZAKA for twenty years.

Shlomo Gotliv – Commander of ZAKA Modi'in Illit and a volunteer in the organization for over twenty years.

Jamal Warraqy – Israeli-Muslim, a ZAKA volunteer for thirteen years.

The photographs in this book were taken in the days following the terrorist attack. They are not necessarily directly related to the events described.

Photography: Zohar Shpak, ZAKA Organization.

"A three-year-old child in a kindergarten – a knife was lodged in his head, inside the skull. There was a hammer on the floor next to him – on the hammer itself were pieces of his skull."

"After five days in which I slept a total of five hours, I returned home to rest," **Simcha Greinman**, a ZAKA volunteer for thirty-two years and the organization's international communications speaker, told me.

Simcha worked non-stop since the Black Sabbath of October 7th and returned home to honor the Sabbath afterward, but on Friday morning, he was called back to Kibbutz Be'eri with his team.

"We arrived at the kibbutz around 11:00, but they did not let us in as soon as we arrived. There was no voice and no answer. The shooting was crazy, non-stop." Simcha did not give up and turned to an IDF officer who was there. "Listen to me well," he scolded him to get his attention during the inferno. Simcha told him insistently that there was no chance that he would desecrate the Sabbath for no reason and demanded that he be given work. The officer was convinced and directed him to check burned buildings that Israeli forces had not yet entered. One of them was a nursery and a kindergarten that belonged to Kibbutz Be'eri.

"I entered the building and saw a small mound at the end of the corridor. I called my team to come and lift the concrete in the area. I had a strange feeling. We found a child, probably five or six years old, when we lifted the concrete. It was possible to know this only by the structure of his jaw because he was all burned, from bottom to top. Everything. Burned. Completely."

Simcha told me with great difficulty that not only was the child burned, but the ceiling above him collapsed, and he was left among the ruins. But to Simcha's and the team's great sorrow, this was far from the end of the story.

"We continued to the second room in that kindergarten, where we found a very small three or four-year-old child. We witnessed a very, very shocking scene. He had a knife stuck in his head, inside the skull. On the floor was a hammer whose handle was completely burned, and on the hammer itself were pieces of the toddler's skull. We put both children into bags."

In my great innocence, I turned to Simcha and tried to find out if there were adults who stayed in the building. Simcha told me that he and the team searched for the responsible adult who was there, who probably watched over those children before and during the inferno, but they did not find him.

"When we continued to search the house, what we did find was a terrorist's vest with the Kalashnikov lying next to it. We ran out of the building quickly and informed the IDF that the building had not been cleared at all. In retrospect, it turned out that there were five terrorists in the building."

Simcha told me that this event had an impact on him, so he insisted on finding out who else was in the building and sent his team to check that specific building time and time again. Just before Simcha told me what the team discovered, and while I was looking at his grim face, I thought to myself, it can't get any worse than this. Two children were murdered and burned. Pieces of a baby's, toddler's skull were left scorched on the heart of the hammer.

Per my request at the beginning of the interview, Simcha did not spare any details.

"We found two more people and scattered bones. I brought a special unit of pathologists into the building to examine and scan it. When I returned to Be'eri the next time, there was no longer a building, no rooms, and no children. But yes, besides the children, we found two more people and scattered bones."

I took a deep breath - another testimony out of dozens that I was exposed to in recent months.

Another testimony that undermined my faith in humanity.

Once again, in my innocence, I turned to Simcha with a question and hoped to hear the correct answer. Unfortunately, I was disappointed again.

"Simcha, I'm sorry for asking, but the knife in the child's skull, I assume he, was also burned. Is it known if the terrorists stuck the knife and the hammer in him while he was alive or only afterward?" I asked in a dull voice.

"Probably it was when he was alive. I don't think they stuck a knife in his skull when he was no longer alive. From what I saw, everything was done together while abusing and dealing with the children. Yes, they were alive when they were abused, both of them," he answered.

"They put a live grenade in her hand so she wouldn't move and raped her. We found her bent forward, naked and shot. In another building, there were thirty bodies, most of them naked women. There is no doubt that there was a massive rape there."

Simcha continued to talk about the inferno that took place in Kibbutz Be'eri, and the horrors he experienced at the blood-filled kibbutz were far from over.

"From the kindergarten where we found the two children, one burned and the other burned with pieces of the skull outside, we continued to buildings number 46 and 47. They warned us in advance that on the left side of the buildings, there was still a terrorist hiding with a vest and grenades on him and that in the center of the building, there was a very, very sharp smell."

The warnings did not prevent Simcha and his team from continuing. They entered the building, immediately saw a piece of tin, and moved it. A mattress was revealed before their eyes.

"We cut the mattress and managed to pull half of it out of the way, and then we saw a woman bent forward, naked. We dug around her to extract her body. While we were taking out her body, we found another body underneath. It was also naked."

Since there were two civilian bodies, not a terrorist body, I had no choice but to ask Simcha.

"I'm sorry for asking. Were they a couple that was killed while having sex, or are we talking about rape?"

Simcha paused for a few seconds, took deep breaths, and answered, "This is not for us to check. We are not pathologists, but yes, these are civilian bodies."

After he answered, I wondered if it could be a couple that just wanted to fulfill their love. But how could it be when the couple knew that outside, there was an inferno that had never been seen before? Did they feel death, and instead of hiding, did they decide to be together in the last moments? Did they not know or were not exposed to what was happening? Were the terrorists who invaded the kibbutz the ones who forced them to have sex and then murdered the couple?

I immediately understood that this could be one of many events for which we will probably never get complete, straightforward answers to.

Simcha continued his testimony and shook me even more, "In this building, they found thirty more bodies, most of them women, and all of them were naked."

It was inevitable for me to interrupt and ask, "That is, there is no choice but to conclude that there was rape there, maybe even group rape."

This time, Simcha had no doubt, "Definitely. Definitely, when you see these things, there is no doubt about them. There was rape there."

In another house in Kibbutz Be'eri, one of the main slaughter centers of the disaster that befell the State of Israel, Simcha said that he was exposed to more horrors.

"We found a woman who was bent forward on the bed. Her lower body was naked, and as we were approaching to turn her over to extract the body, we found a grenade in her hand, without the pin. They shot her in the head. Here there were no doubts whether she was raped or not raped. In the pose, she was lying, and with an active grenade in her hand, there is no doubt."

Although I am already twenty-three years old and define myself as someone who has been through a lot in his life, I immediately stopped Simcha.

"So why did they put a grenade in her hand if they shot her eventually?"

Even now, in retrospect, I do not know why I asked this. Am I so naive, or perhaps I am trying to deny the incomprehensible reality that was right before my eyes?

Simcha answered simply and with chilling composure, "So she wouldn't move. While they were raping her, they trapped her in such a way that if she moved, it would explode. They knew she wouldn't want to die, so they put her in that situation."

He emphasized that fortunately for him and the team, the grenade did not explode.

"In one second, it could have exploded on us. Her hand could have opened in a second, and the grenade could have slipped. We laid her back and ran out."

"There were twenty three Thai citizens whose remains were found in a huge pool of blood. They slit their throats, shot their legs. In fact, we walked into a pool of blood. The terrorists slaughtered them all. They drained their blood, like slaughtering a chicken with knives and hammers."

Not only Israeli citizens were slaughtered in Hamas's terrorist attack. The terrorists did not distinguish between types of blood.

They slaughtered civilians from Brazil, Argentina, and Colombia, from the United States and Canada, from Russia, Australia, and Cambodia. Of course, they also did not pass over Europeans; the victims also came from Britain, France, Germany, and many other countries. In fact, every continent on the globe (except uninhabited Antarctica) suffered casualties in the attack, whether murdered, kidnapped, injured, or missing.

"I arrived at the dining room, in the kitchenette of the foreign Thai workers," Simcha told me. "There was a kind of step at the entrance to the room. The moment I passed the step, I fell into a puddle." Since the place was utterly dark, Simcha and the team lit flashlights. They will never forget what was found there. "We found a puddle of blood... a puddle? That was not a puddle. The whole room was flooded with blood! Just in this dining room, there were seven Thais who were slaughtered, blood drained from their bodies."

"Wait, what does that mean, 'blood drained from their bodies'?" I asked gently and feared the answer.

"They shot them in the legs and then slaughtered them like slaughtering a chicken. They took off their heads just like that. The head was not completely decapitated, but they slit their throats, and the people simply bled to death. With knives and axes, whatever they had, whatever was at their disposal."

Simcha told how he coped with the hard scene he found.

"Luckily, I found a pile of rice bags in the kitchenette. I took a box cutter, cut open the rice bags, and used the rice to absorb the blood. So much blood. It was completely insane - crazy amounts of blood. I'm telling you, we couldn't step on the floor. It was one giant pool of blood! We had to pour between twelve and thirteen bags of rice so we wouldn't slip in this blood. You can only conclude from this - the abuse that was there was terrible."

The last sentence forced me to turn to Simcha and clarify, "Is there any indication whether they abused them before they murdered them or afterward?"

Simcha did not hesitate and replied, "It was during the killing. They shot them in the legs before they murdered them. We know this because, according to the shooting, there was an entrance and exit of the bullet from the leg, so they could not escape. Then they approached them and slit their throats to finish the job. They were murdered in such a disgusting way. It was horrifying."

Natan Kenig, a ZAKA volunteer for twenty-eight years, asked not to forget the foreign victims of the attack.

"True, the terrorists came upon the Jewish people living in Zion, but they did not care who they were murdering or discriminating. They killed Egyptians, Japanese, Italians, Russians, Thais. The list is much longer, and I apologize to the nations whose names I did not mention."

"Five family members huddled in a circle. The children grabbed their parents by the legs, the heads of the parents and the grandmother leaned on each other. It's a wonderful family picture. Only everyone was burned."

Simcha mainly talked about his work a week after the attack. But he was there from the first moment.

"I entered Kibbutz Be'eri with my team. It was already the evening of Sunday, October 8th. We entered one of the houses at night. We managed to extract two bodies, but there was a frenzy of shooting inside the kibbutz, and they quickly kicked us out of there."

But Simcha and his team did not intend to leave so quickly and waited nearby until dawn.

"All night, there was a tough battle in Be'eri. We stood there like chickens. The shooting left us in terrible fear. I was not prepared for something like that."

Finally, the IDF and armed forces gave Simcha and his team permission to enter the houses in Be'eri.

"We entered one house; I opened the door, and a birthday cake was standing on the table before me." Simcha shared with me that the moment he noticed the cake. He had already thought about the scenario differently. He began to wonder if it was indeed a birthday cake. And if so, then whose? Did the celebrants survive? Or is it perhaps a 'Simhat Torah[1]' cake?

He admitted that his thoughts were distracted for a few seconds, and he tried searching for pictures of the family members on the

---

1. A Jewish holiday that celebrates and marks the conclusion of the annual cycle of public Torah readings, and the beginning of a new cycle.

fridge to understand what the story was and what it was about. "It caught my attention; there was no escape. But I didn't come to eat cake; I came to take care of the bodies," he said. "Immediately, the sharp, burnt smell of the shelter caught our attention. We entered the room and saw five family members. Two children, a pair of parents and a grandmother. All five were hugging each other in a circle. The children held their parents by the legs, and the heads of the parents and the grandmother leaned on each other."

"Were they all burned?" I stopped him mid-sentence as if I were someone who was just looking for answers.

"They were all burned, yes. Completely burned, everything, everyone," he replied and repeated himself with great grief.

In the intensity of the conversation, I cut him off again. "Were they burned while they were alive?"

With his typical composure, he replied, "Yes. Apparently, they were burned alive since the whole room around them was completely burned and charred, and they were burned from the inside out. Their backs were burned more than their fronts. They just tried to escape the fire by holding and protecting each other, so yes, they were burned while they were alive."

Simcha told me he called that event "circle of life" because they seemed to be hugging and holding each other in a circle.

"The difficulty there was the strongest because, in those moments, we are in a crazy situation. We were the ones who needed to break this circle. We were actually forced to pull out the small hands of the children who held their parents' legs in fear and to separate the heads of the adults who protected each other. We felt like we were the ones who were breaking the family circle," he shared. "We, as ZAKA volunteers, had to break this circle and put them into bags."

The mental difficulty did not end there for Simcha and his team.

"As we placed each family member into a bag, we had to carry them outside the house and, on the way, passed in front of the birthday cake with each and every one of them. We were holding in our hands a bag that once contained a human being and experienced once more the scenario in which you try to belong between the cake to the very body bag that you're holding."

When I tried to find out how old the children were, he said, "Young. I can't say what their exact ages were because they were burned and their limbs shrank, but they were two small children."

"And to whom did the cake belong to?" I asked in an attempt to find an ending to the story.

Like most of the answers we have from the events of October 7th, the response remained vague.

"As a ZAKA volunteer, there are things I do, and there are things I don't do. The moment you get attached to a family and enter their story, and you connect to it - the difficulty to get out of it is much greater, and you keep it with you for many years."

Yet, in the current case, Simcha did not resist the temptation.

"I admit, I tried to find a little more information. But to a certain extent, I stopped myself before finding out the family's story. So no, I don't know to whom the cake belonged."

To highlight the dangers of becoming emotionally attached to a family you've worked with, Simcha shared the story of his friend **Moti Bukchin**, the spokesman for ZAKA.

"He collapsed, he just collapsed. This is after he dealt with the Kotz family, followed their story very closely, and took it very personally. The more he dealt with it, the harder it became for him." Simcha summed up, "So I know what my limits are. I know what I can't stand. What will cause me nightmares and unbearable pain? There I stop. But who knows? Maybe in a few months, it will change."

"In Kfar Aza, a tiny baby lay, more precisely, what was left of him. It is unclear whether they first cut off his hands and then beheaded him with an ax or beheaded him and then abused his body – we don't know what was done first."

I encountered the greatest cruelty as we arrived at the kibbutzim on the second and third days. For example, in Kfar Aza, **Ephraim Greidinger**, a ZAKA volunteer for thirty years, told me, "Their method was coming to the houses and demanding that the residents who were in the safe rooms get out. If the residents do not comply, they simply set the houses on fire."

During the dozens of testimonies I was flooded with in recent months, I tried not only to listen and absorb what happened but also to understand how things worked and find logic in the madness.

I turned to the volunteers and asked in horrifying naivety, "I don't understand. Explain how it happens. When you mention burned bodies that are fused together, what does that entail? Do you understand what happened to them at that moment? How are bodies burned together? How is a person's body completely burned so that nothing is left of it? If there are severed legs, can you see if it's from an ax or a knife? How does it work?"

Natan answered that question. "Alon, if you try to find some logic, you won't find it. They didn't try just to kill. They wanted to destroy, and in some cases, they also managed to destroy any possibility of humanity thriving, the possibility that a father, brother, child, or son would come to cry at the grave of his beloved. They also destroyed that."

I was unsatisfied with the answer and continued to insist, "But how did they destroy? How can a person's body be erased?" After all, as

I described in this testimony, Ephraim told me about the houses that were set on fire in Kfar Aza.

Natan was very clear and answered in a way that could not be misinterpreted.

"They were equipped with combustible materials, and they did everything so that no memories of their victims would remain. They layered combustible materials on top of combustible materials, not just to kill but to ensure that not a trace of that person would remain. Just imagine what happens to a person's body in this situation. Some bodies have been reduced to tiny pieces. There are also scenes where nothing is left. Not one thing. In the past, in the most bizarre cases, we managed to find teeth, bones, and things you can extract DNA from. However, this time, there are cases where no trace of DNA exists."

I did not have time to reply to that complex testimony when Natan raised his voice with an undeniable rage and said, "They've tried to eliminate, destroy, kill all human remains and traces."

We returned to what happened in Kibbutz Kfar Aza, and although I could see on his face that he did not want to continue talking about it, I had to find out.

"And what happened to those who did agree to leave the safe rooms?" I asked Ephraim.

"As I said, the greatest horrors I have witnessed took place in the kibbutzim. The terrorists tortured those who left the shelters," he said.

I asked him to describe how so.

"There were axes there. At first, I thought they belonged to the residents who tried to defend themselves. But very quickly, I understood the situation. The terrorists just took an ax and cut a child," he described while demonstrating to me the chopping motion.

"Cut a child?" I asked.

"Yes, there were no gunshot marks anywhere on that child. Only cuts all over the body," he replied. "A three-month-old or half-year-old baby that they cut with an ax in the neck and beheaded, that's after they hit him in the head. His hands were also cut off. It is unclear whether they first cut off his hands and then beheaded him with the ax or beheaded him and then mutilated his body. It is unclear what came first. What is certain is that during the torture, the amputations, and the blows, the baby was alive and felt everything since there were no gunshot marks. That is, whether they first cut off his head or whether his hand, in any case, the murder was done by cutting off his limbs with an ax, so he was alive and felt it."

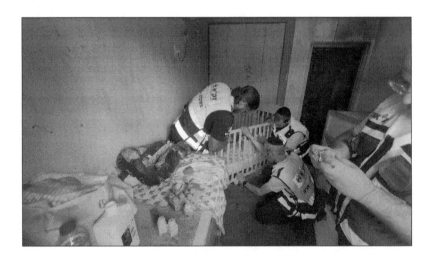

"Was it an isolated and unique case? Or have you experienced similar cases? How often and at what ages?" I asked.

Ephraim looked surprised at the question and even chuckled a bit.

"Do you think what I'm describing is unique or unusual? Do you think it was rare? Not at all. There were many like that child aged eight and nine, two and three. Hey, everyone went through the torture I just described. The terrorists did not have weapons, so they came with axes. Some of the children were hit in the head, some in the rest of the body."

Without much time to digest the images in my mind, I turned to Ephraim and asked calmly, "What do you do with the body of a three-month-old baby whose head is in one place and the other parts of the body are elsewhere?"

"Put in a bag," Ephraim replied sharply and continued, "We separate between the head and the rest of the body because we cannot be sure it belongs to the same person, or the same baby, or child. But we do note that the body parts were found near the severed head. There is an orderly procedure with bags."

"In what other ways did they kill people?" I asked Ephraim, who did not hesitate to tell me that in addition to people being burned and tortured with axes and knives, there were people who were strangled with zip ties.

"A very primitive and easy method. There were burnt people who were also tied up, strangled and choked with barbwire. Apparently, they wanted to take them captive and failed, so they just burned them," he revealed.

I sat and thought about that choice.

A choice that a rational human mind cannot grasp.

A cruel choice that even the devil did not create but was indeed made consciously by Hamas's terrorists.

The choice facing the kibbutz residents, intact families, parents, and their children at that moment was whether to remain in the protected compounds and be burned, or to suffocate to death while still alive, as has been described and will be further described in this book. Alternatively, the other option was for them to leave the protected and enclosed rooms, and to endure abuse, including a slow and cruel death by dismemberment with saws and knives.

There were many cruel choices that faced the kibbutz residents during those tragic moments in front of whole families, parents, and their children. The choice to stay in the protected areas and burn or to be strangled to death while still alive is already described and will be detailed in later testimonies in this book. The choice to perhaps leave the safe rooms, the shelters, and the protected spaces and undergo torture that included a slow and cruel death by dismemberment with axes and knives? What is the point of making a choice if the outcome is the same?

"I saw smashed heads and amputated body parts, people who were tied up and burned. A seventy five year old man who had his limbs cut off in all parts of his body, a foreign worker who had her head torn off by stepping on it with a foot."

"The things I saw there, you wouldn't see in horror movies or even in movies about the Holocaust. Movies don't come close to what I saw. They really don't come close to it," **Reuven**, who has been working at ZAKA as a vehicle and logistics manager for twenty years, told me. "We've been through a lot at ZAKA but never experienced things like this. Smashed heads, amputations, it's just unimaginably horrifying."

I tried to find out where Reuven was mainly exposed to the horrors he described, and he immediately used Kibbutz Be'eri as an example. He told me about the dental clinic belonging to the kibbutz, where, according to him, mainly children, but also adults, escaped from the inferno.

"There was a battle there. Two adults tried to protect the doors and windows, and in the end, the terrorists just threw some grenades, blew up the place, and shot all the children."

Reuven said that even though the terrorists had already blown up all the glass and managed to invade the clinic and harm the children, it was not enough for them. According to him, their game was to pass child after child, shoot a bullet in their head, and move on.

With faint hope, I nevertheless tried to extract some optimistic information from Reuven, some kind of miracle that happened in the clinic.

"So, they just killed all the children?" I asked as I prayed for some good news.

"All the children who were in the clinic were murdered. No one survived. There were seven children there, and we took out seven bodies. They were all murdered."

I asked him to tell me why the children went to the dental clinic, of all places, in the midst of the inferno. He explained that it seemed that they simply fled there to survive, which, in the end, was far from reality.

I am the youngest sibling in my family, and I have four beloved nephews. They are dear to my heart, and without them, my world would be completely different.

I felt the need to find out the ages of the children who were in the clinic and more general information about these murdered children.

"From the age of zero to the age of one hundred. There is no age here. We met all ages. Babies, toddlers, children, adults, the elderly. They spared no one. Anyone they couldn't kidnap or didn't interest them, they simply murdered. They murdered in cold blood. There is not one house they did not burn."

The tragedy of Kibbutz Be'eri did not end at the clinic. Not by a long shot.

"When I arrived at one of the houses in the kibbutz, I saw an elderly man, probably around the age of seventy-five. They simply cut off all his body parts, threw a grenade at him and left. The first thing they did was abuse him. That was their game, their fun."

Instinctively and out of unfortunate curiosity, I asked Reuven if the abuse of that elderly man he was talking about took place. At the same time, he was alive, and Reuven nodded his head.

"Yes, he was alive, and I believe he was killed with an ax, according to the marks on his body."

When I tried to find out which parts of the body were cut, he refused to answer specifically but stated, "They cut off all his body parts."

I insisted on understanding the circumstances of the incident, and Reuven gave me some more information.

"They cut off his body parts. Tied him up in the safe room, cut up his body, threw a grenade and left."

The hellish sights did not end for him.

"On the second or third day after the massacre, we found a woman hiding under the bed." Reuven, who immediately asked her how she was, said that the woman replied that she was fine, but she had a hard time dealing mentally with what was done to her foreign employee.

"After calming her down, I went into the house and saw what happened. It was horrifying."

"What did you see?" I asked, trying to understand the details of the incident, but Reuven still faced the horrors.

"It's hard for me to tell this, very hard for me." After a few seconds of silence, he chose to continue. "They cut off her head by stomping on it, not with an axe."

I tried to picture the event in my mind, but I couldn't really do it.

"Is that something that can even be done?" I asked.

Reuven replied that it turns out that whoever is cruel enough can.

"We just saw the marks of the footprints and realized what happened."

In an attempt to obtain more details and preserve that foreign worker's memory and, of course, to commemorate what happened,

I had to keep insisting. Some would say that I even lacked sensitivity.

"The stomping of a foot cut the head off?" I turned to Reuven with concern.

"The head was cut off from the body, yes. Part of it was torn with a persistent stomp of a foot. You can see the cruelty toward the victim," he said.

"Only someone deep inside could have obtained such intelligence for them. They came with neat records, pages, maps, addresses, videos of buildings and instructions on who to kill first."

"They didn't feel sorry for us; they didn't show any mercy. They 'attacked' us in every possible way using axes, knives, everything," Reuven said. He also added that the Hamas terrorists planned everything carefully and were waiting for the IDF, the national forces, the ZAKA volunteers, and the MDA to attack them as well.

"They hid grenades for us in refrigerators, drawers, everywhere possible so that we too would become victims. Thank God, so far, a miracle has saved us. The grenades were simply waiting for us everywhere imaginable, above and below doors, entrances, closets, and under mattresses."

"What do you mean under the mattresses?" I asked.

Reuven said that he and his team found a woman lying down. They picked her up, and under her, they found a grenade that, according to him, was intended to hurt the forces that would arrive later. In another incident he handled, a small boy was found tied up with a grenade next to him. According to him, everything was carefully planned, and the terrorists laid traps for those who would come to treat the wounded bodies.

Since October 7th, the State of Israel has been in total shock. A heavy fog hovers over dozens of questions regarding not only the readiness of the IDF and the national forces - but also the readiness of Hamas and the time it devoted to that exact, meticulously planned attack, which, regrettably, they considered successful. This attack caught the Israeli security agencies off guard in a failure that was unprecedented since the nation's founding.

For the first time since the beginning of the series of testimonies, a representative of ZAKA spoke with me about the extraordinary, precise plan that the terrorist organization had before the attack on October 7th and tried to answer some of the mysterious questions to which the citizens of Israel have not yet received answers to.

"They had a list of who should be killed first. The rest of the victims were just a bonus. First of all, they were looking for the security officers, the members of the standby classes, and the police. They had amazingly accurate maps of where everyone lived, and not only that. They knew how many cartridges each had, how many guns each had at home, and where they hid them. Beyond that - they knew where the entrances and exits from the houses were."

"Where do you get such accurate intelligence?" I asked Reuven, trying to understand the magnitude of the failure.

"It could only happen if it was someone on the inside, very deep inside. Someone who hung around there day and night," he answered.

"Who was it?" I had to find out.

Reuven told me about a man named Khalil, who worked at Kibbutz Be'eri and gave Hamas all this information.

"I don't know that the story is verified, but I believe someone did it. It is someone who collected a lot of information over a long period of time and gave that information to Hamas. This is about gathering intelligence over a long period from within Israeli territory. It is not something you find in two minutes," he noted.

I tried to find out more about Khalil.

"Did he have a work permit? Did he enter Israel illegally?"

Reuven confidently answered, "He has worked here as a gardener for thirty years. The name "Khalil" was mentioned frequently by both volunteers and locals, who were very familiar with him and noted his cooperation with Hamas."

Reuven did not stop there. It seemed that the more he talked about the issue, the greater the failure and the anger accumulated. "There is no way that a terrorist arrives with an exact list, with house numbers, people's numbers, the number of weapons they stockpile, which standby class someone is in, and at what time he leaves and returns home. There is no chance of such a thing happening unless it is someone who is on the inside, and not just anyone, someone who is deep inside, not a random person."

I insisted on verifying.

"Where did this information come from that allowed terrorists access to records and addresses of houses?"

Reuven did not hesitate.

"What does that mean? I saw it myself on the bodies of the terrorists. I saw terrorists who had records and maps in their pockets, terrorists who came with binoculars, terrorists who had marked on pages what to do, where and when." He added, "This was an act of planned terror. To see all the holes they made in the fences, all the looting and mess they made in the houses, they definitely knew what they were doing. The moment you open a refrigerator and you see a grenade lying there, you will understand how prepared they were for this. It was not something they had planned at the last minute; the traps were not in one house. They were in all the houses, everywhere it was carefully planned."

Reuven did not know how to answer my question about what finally happened to Khalil.

"I don't know, but I would love to participate in his funeral."

"They confirmed the baby's death. Over forty bullets in the body of a little boy. Forty bullets! They tied people up and cut them, burned them, chopped them."

When I started interviewing **Shlomo Gotliv**, commander of ZAKA Modi'in Elite and a volunteer with the organization for over twenty years, I shared my feelings that the testimony he was about to give actually constituted a "Zikaron Basalon[2]" of the October 7th Holocaust. This remark did not go unnoticed by Shlomo, who had a hard time hiding his feelings.

"Wow, you gave me the chills right now. You have no idea how much."

When I asked him why my remark affected him so much, I realized that he had come to testify with a firm opinion, and some would say controversial, but one that was important for him to convey.

"You gave me chills just now when you said it like that. As part of my various duties, I am also a tour guide and lead trips to Poland. During the week of the Black Sabbath, friends from the delegations to Poland asked me, 'What can you say about that? Look at this: we went through a holocaust.' I turned to them and unambiguously told them: 'Listen to me carefully. While we understand that there are people who want their homes back—a population that wants its houses, settlements that want their homes, and families that want their houses and gardens—we must remember that there are people here who need to know what happened. In their current state, these homes serve as museums and commemorate the attack. Therefore, they should not be restored by the country.'"

---

2. An initiative of people who decided to take action and create a new way – more intimate, meaningful and accessible – to keep the memory of the Holocaust alive.

Shlomo wanted to convey a clear message to the Israeli government and the parties involved.

"If the state begins to put everyone's house in order again, then in fact, we, as the State of Israel, will remain the number one holocaust deniers of October 7th." He continued, "Even the stories of the Holocaust could become "imaginary stories" two hundred years from now if what exists today in Poland does not remain as a memorial. And we must not allow that to happen here. We must not make it so that we can deny what happened by looking ahead. When I am told that the kibbutz residents want to return to normal life in their homes, I say to myself, Lord of the world, God all Mighty - what will happen next? How will the memory be preserved?"

When I insisted on hearing his opinion about those people who just want to return to their homes, he said, "On the one hand, I say they deserve their homes. They are precious people. They deserve to live. On the other hand, I'm sure they also want their grandchildren to know what happened. So, it must be documented lest we end up in a situation where someone denies this horrific event."

In general, Shlomo's testimony was emotional. Right at the beginning of the conversation, when I turned to him and told him that for me, the ZAKA volunteers are the ones who did holy work for the State of Israel, Shlomo stopped me.

"It's important for me to tell you something. You are such a nice guy, but you said something that bothered and upset me, so I'm stopping you right now." Shlomo emphasized the importance of documentation and memory for the future and talked about the country's current state of unity: "'There is no such thing as 'us and you.' We are all here together in the country. There are the IDF soldiers who do their job properly, the ZAKA volunteers who wonderfully do their job, and you, as a writer, are working on writing a book that will be distributed to the world and will show everyone what happened. So, from this moment on, it's not you. It's us together because if we don't understand it, we will live as several nations within one nation. We are one people and one heart, and only with that we move forward."

Shlomo told me how naively the Black Sabbath began for him.

"I was observing the Sabbath[3]. My brother came home in the morning and asked me if I knew what was happening in the South. He told me about a party where hundreds of people were murdered."

Really? To Shlomo, his brother's news did not sound credible, and he believed that even if an incident did occur in the South, it was of a magnitude that MDA could handle.

"I pushed it aside. It didn't sound realistic to me. We continued to drink as a mitzva of the "Simhat Torah" holiday."

The second time, after he arrived for the mid-day prayer at the synagogue, a member of the stand-by squad turned to him and said, "There are hundreds of dead."

Shlomo remained skeptical.

"Stop with your imagination!" he ordered.

His naivete did not stop even the third time.

"At the synagogue, some people talked about canceling the second lap of Torah Rejoice because of what is happening. And I said, what? To cancel second laps? Who would allow such a thing?"

---

3. To cease our work life and break our daily routine every seventh day, making that day holy.

Shlomo had his walkie-talkies off as well as all means of communication because of the Shabbat.

"As soon as I turned the phone on at the end of Shabbat, I was filled with shock and sorrow," he said.

He began to realize that he was wrong. He began to realize that the worst had indeed happened, and he was not there to help.

The next day, he set off.

His naivete was still not lost when he passed between Roads 232 and 34, the infernal roads in the South.

"I didn't understand how rockets might have caused such severe damage between the two sides of the road. I also assumed that all the dozens of abandoned cars I saw on the road belonged to women who were afraid of the sirens and, out of stress, had gotten into a big accident. I'm telling you this and laughing at myself because I couldn't get it into my head that something else was happening. For a moment, I didn't understand at all that there was a war raging, that this was a battlefield, that in this place, there were actually terrorists who murdered people and who burned these cars."

But when he arrived at Kibbutz Be'eri, there was no more room for naivete.

"Under hellish conditions, we went inside. We went from house to house and saw what happened."

Shlomo said that one of the volunteers in his team came to him and told him about parents and a child who he found burned in their home.

"Put them each in a separate bag," he ordered.

Only a few minutes passed, and another volunteer from the team he commanded came out of one of the houses with a baby in his hand.

"They made sure the baby was dead," the volunteer wailed.

Shlomo still maintained his characteristic composure and tried to encourage his friend.

"Shlomo, you don't understand what this is about. It's not just a confirmation of death," the volunteer shouted at him, "there are over forty bullets in the body of a little boy!"

At that moment, Shlomo broke down.

The naivete he had disappeared and his soul was deeply wounded.

"We just cried together."

The horrific condition of the baby's body touched that volunteer, prompting him to ask to be the one to take the baby's bag to the refrigerated trucks.

Like Reuven, who told about the massacre that took place in the dental clinic in Be'eri, his friend Shlomo also did not remain indifferent to the case.

"When I arrived at the clinic, there were so many dead in such a small place. I found myself taking out a body and hugging it. I couldn't act otherwise. Yes, I hugged corpses."

After the volunteers removed the seven children who were murdered in the clinic, this was in addition to other residents who were murdered in Be'eri, as well as the baby who was shot over forty times, they held a march with about fifteen bodies toward the refrigerated trucks.

This was actually their last march.

"We paid them our respects and held one big funeral for them. We put all the bodies side by side and held a funeral for them exactly as it should be with blessings, Kaddish and all the other customs."

On the same day that Gotliv and his friends removed approximately fifteen bodies, another sixty bodies were removed from Kibbutz Be'eri.

"It was Be'eri's big day," Gotliv said with chilling sarcasm, trying to deal with the horrors humorously. "When I got home, I refused to tell the family what I saw because I didn't want to get it into my head," he said.

With great difficulty but with no choice, I turned to him, "How did they kill people there?"

There were a few seconds of silence in the room; Shlomo was probably thinking of how to respond.

"I'll explain something to you," he began, "the reason I'm willing to talk to you at all, and that I've talked to you until now, is because of what you said at the beginning that it's for memory. And if it's for memory, I'll make the supernatural effort against my nature just because I think it should be done, and we should talk about it."

I didn't answer, and Shlomo continued.

"To answer your question, how did they kill people there? It's true that everything is confused and jumbled for me because I tried hard not to let it in my head, but I saw shootings, I saw beheadings, I saw cuttings, I saw tying up, I saw amputations. I saw everything. When I say I saw everything, I saw that people were tied up, so they suffocated. They were cut. And I saw people who were burned, even though they were also tied up. And I saw a father and a mother who were just trying to protect their child, and they were both killed. There was also a situation where the child was above the father. I don't know what happened there, under what circumstances they were murdered."

Shlomo shared another testimony from Kfar Aza.

"We were about to leave the kibbutz after finishing work there. A car parked there, and a man got out, not protected in any way. I tried to explain to him that the place was under attack, but he refused to listen to me. I insisted, but he waved me off. I tried to find out if he was local, and he pointed to his house. The house was all destroyed and burned."

Shlomo said the local guy summed up the horrors he experienced in one sentence.

In a weak voice, the man told him, "There's nothing to return for."

"Six family members who simply became one block when they were burned while still alive. The baby's body was stuck to his mother's body. The atrocities? They were also committed by the residents of the Gaza Strip themselves."

The interview with ZAKA volunteer **Jamal Warraqy** was challenging to schedule.

It was postponed several times due to urgent ZAKA events, including a fatal car accident.

Even when we met, Jamal was in an ambulance after a long work day. During the testimony, we had to stop due to calls coming in from the organization's liaison about an active shooter nearby.

Jamal has been a ZAKA volunteer for thirteen years, an Israeli-Muslim who, like others, witnessed the atrocities of October 7th.

While wearing a necklace bearing the message 'bring our hostages back,' he said, "When we arrived at the festival, and then the kibbutz, my nightmare began. Everything I thought I had seen in my life turned out to be nothing compared to what I experienced in the South. Bodies that were burned, families were burned, people had their limbs cut off, and houses that were set on fire. There were corpses everywhere, no matter where I looked. There wasn't a house I passed that didn't have at least one corpse in it. They really abused them and their corpses as well."

"Can you elaborate on what it means that they were abused?" I asked Jamal.

He told me that at the Re'im festival, he did not come across a single body that did not have a confirmation of death with a bullet in the head. According to him, everyone, absolutely everyone at the party, had been shot in the head. He went on to talk about Kfar

Aza as well, "Everyone who was murdered was also burned. Most of the bodies I found were cuffed with their hands behind their backs, and the meaning is simple: before they were killed, they were simply abused, even children and the helpless elderly."

"How were they abused?" I insisted on hearing the whole truth from him.

"I saw an entire family that was burned while still alive, to the extent that six bodies became one mass. We could not distinguish one body from another because they were burned to the core. We tried to locate the baby in the family, and his body was stuck to his mother's body, probably because they were burned alive. Apparently, the mother just hugged her baby while they were burned together. From one mass of charcoal, we had to start understanding who the child was and who the father was. It seems that some of the children in that family held their parents while they were being burned, and one of them was also in the middle between the parents."

Jamal said that every time he thought he had seen the worst, the following scene managed to surprise him.

Like Reuven, he also testified that Hamas's terrorists booby-trapped bodies.

"I was treating a resident who was shot, and I recognized a charge under the shirt. Grenades were hidden under the cavities. They were waiting for us to arrive and for the traps to be activated. It was like this with almost everybody we treated."

Jamal did not skimp on the details either and shared some insights into this scene as well.

"The massacre that took place was indeed carried out by the Nohba terrorists (Ezz ad-Din al-Qassam Brigades), but the atrocities that were carried out were done by the Gaza residents who entered after them. I'm talking about the rape, the abuse, the looting."

Since this is the first time I have heard that the residents of Gaza were also the ones who participated in the atrocities, at least broadly as described by Jamal, I had to find out.

"Wait, then explain to me the difference between the activities of the Nohba and the activities of the residents of Gaza," I asked.

"The Nohba did the shooting, the massacre itself. But the real abuse was carried out by residents."

I asked one more time to make sure.

"Gaza residents who entered through the gaps in the fence and abused the residents?"

He nodded and replied. "They entered with the Hamas terrorists together through the gaps in the fence." Immediately afterward, Jamal said something that I had never heard, even from the Jewish ZAKA volunteers, "At that moment, you realize what kind of people you are dealing with."

Jamal also compared the events of October 7th to the Holocaust, "You can't even call it 'inhuman,' the things that were there. It doesn't describe it well enough. I don't think there is a word that would describe it well enough. Maybe it is actually a Holocaust. This nation endured another Holocaust. We used to remember the Holocaust, and now we remember both the Holocaust and October 7th. The abuse, the burnings - they tried to make Holocaust number 2."

Jamal's declaration when he mentioned the Palestinian people got stuck in my head, and I could not avoid asking, "Especially as an Israeli-Muslim, when you say that you understand 'what kind of people you are dealing with,' who do you mean? Hamas? Jihad? The people of Gaza? Palestinian people in general?"

Jamal did not hesitate.

"I'm talking about Hamas and everything that surrounds it. Hamas are not only fighters. Hamas are also citizens and residents who support Hamas. Anyone who supports this thing is simply inhuman. As a Muslim person, I tell you the religion of Islam has nothing to do with what happened there. They murdered everyone. It didn't interest them at all. Muslims, Arabs, and drivers from East Jerusalem were shot in the head. A pregnant Bedouin woman was also shot at. There was another woman who saved her husband and her baby, who was less than a year old, by hiding in an electrical cabinet for hours, waiting for the Israeli forces to arrive."

His unequivocal and unhesitating support forced me to ask, "So how do you explain that there are several Israeli citizens, Israeli-Muslims like you, who support the atrocities of Hamas?"

Jamal told me the answer is simple.

For him, those who support Hamas simply do not know the extent of the horror.

"Until now, people do not fully understand what happened. The world does not understand what happened. If a video was released on behalf of the state showing what we saw, I doubt if anyone would be able to continue supporting them. No rational person who comprehends the scale of what happened can support it."

As he said this, I could only think to myself, maybe this book will contribute to the exact cause he is talking about.

Following the extraordinary support, I asked him about two in-state issues, issues within Israel, which apparently should concern us as a society.

"And after the sacred work you did, and still do, do you feel that you experienced any racism or discrimination from the Jewish public during the war and in general? On the other hand, did your unwavering support for the State of Israel, its bodies and its institutions cause you to be distanced, ostracized, or discriminated against within Israeli Arab society?"

"First of all, regarding the first question, I don't feel any discrimination from my team at ZAKA, neither from the soldiers nor from the police. On the contrary, I only got a look of appreciation from everyone. I am part of this country. But I won't lie; I also happened to encounter racism from a few extremists. During the war, a saleswoman heard me speaking in Arabic on the phone outside the store, and when I entered, she refused to sell me anything."

I could only share with Jamal how much I regret events of this type and wonder at the magnitude of the absurdity in which a man who not only does his sacred work in the ZAKA but also served in the IDF as a combat soldier in the Border Guard Police in active service and reserves, contributed a lot to the country, and identifies first of all as Israeli encountered a horrible attitude from that saleswoman whose values are questionable.

"I have always experienced this racism. It exists, you can't deny it. But I also understand where it comes from. A little girl who was raised to hate Arabs will behave like that even to a good person," Jamal told me. "Regarding your second question about being ostracized from Arab society, so yes, I severed contact with my family back when I was in the army. It is difficult to identify as an Israeli within the Israeli Muslim society. But I am neither afraid nor regretful. I will continue to identify like this. I do not regret anything I did."

I insisted and pressed him, "Even though you lost your family?"

He did not hesitate for a moment.

"Of course, I have no regrets. This is me; this is my identity; I am Israeli. My belief is that you cannot spit on the plate you eat from, like Arabs who identify as Palestinians, but wait every month to receive social security payments from the State of Israel or supermarket employees who support Hamas. Is it not good enough for you? Not satisfied? Go and work in the West Bank."

Jamal also showed empathy towards his family.

"It is important to emphasize my family is not a family of terrorists. They are neutral. But Arab society is built on 'what the others will think and what they will say.' These days, I have a shallow relationship with them, and I am only in touch with my mother. I am not in touch with the rest of the family. Moreover, some of the family sent me derogatory messages during this period. But I don't care."

Following his words, I asked him what his message is to the civilian population in the Gaza Strip these days.

"As an Israeli, I encourage what our army is doing. From a human point of view, of course, my heart aches for the children who are killed there. A large population in Gaza just wants to live in peace. Hamas is a small fraction of the population in Gaza. Golda Meir once said that if the Palestinians loved their children more than they hated our children, there would be peace. It's time for them to start loving their children. Hamas hides behind civilians and shoots from schools. Residents of Gaza - stand up for yourself and stop being afraid of Hamas."

So, back to the horrors.

When Jamal told me that in almost every scene where they found murdered children, volunteers who have been in the organization for decades could not hold back tears, I asked him to tell me how he deals with his mental state.

"Since that day, I'm not the same person. You know what? I won't lie to you. It really affects me negatively. I sink into depression, and I can't concentrate on work lately. It even affects my relationships; I come home and hardly speak or share. At the end of the day, all you want is to cry and fall apart."

Jamal summed up in such a precise and touching way, one that even I, as a writer, have not yet achieved. "The people of Israel learned to die together. Now we have to learn to live together," he added, "from now on, there is no more Arab-Jewish, nonreligious-Orthodox, left-right. It's time to get a grip and maintain free love. This crisis is proof of that."

"You try to decipher it. You see two skulls that are connected to each other and one body. You understand that it is two people. But where is the body of the other person? And to which of the skulls does the body that is in front of us belong?"

"People ask why the terrorists didn't enter Netivot. The legend says that because 'Baba Sali's grave is there - so he actually prevented them from entering," Ephraim told me.

Not only did they not reach Netivot, but they also did not reach Ashdod, Kiryat Gat, Kiryat Malachi and more. According to Ephraim, the reason for this was the heroic acts of the state's citizens, the security forces, and full-fledged individuals whose activities that day prevented the terrorists from reaching further than they did.

"It is important for me to emphasize," Ephraim said, "they (the citizens) had no skills for something like this. They did not prepare for this. They defended with everything they had within reach at that moment. When we arrived at Ofakim early in the morning, we found a 'Duvdevan[4]' soldier who had returned home on leave without his weapon. As soon as he realized what was happening, he took a kitchen knife, stabbed the first terrorist who was there, took the weapon from him and continued to conduct the battle. He went up to the roof of his house and killed about six terrorists whose bodies we found in the street. He fought up until a sniper arrived, a terrorist, and killed him."

He also said that the body of that nineteen-year-old Duvdevan

---

4. An elite military unit dedicated to fighting in various areas and works to prevent terrorist activities.

soldier was taken down from the roof of his apartment by ZAKA volunteers while his family was there.

Ephraim also shared another side of death. Some citizens who witnessed the atrocities, instead of fighting, decided to end their lives rather than fall victim to the brutality of Hamas terrorists.

"In Kfar Aza, I found a body that was hanging from the roof of one of the houses. I don't think they hung it; rather, this guy committed suicide before they arrived. He decided to take a cable and kill himself. He knew the terrorists were coming and decided not to hand himself over to them."

Ephraim contacted me with a special request: to highlight the bright spot he experienced on Route 232, that notorious road of horrors.

"I arrived at a gas station. I didn't understand why a soldier was standing next to the fuel pump as if he were operating it. Well, he fueled my car for free. On top of that, he asked me what I wanted to eat and drink and gave me whatever I needed."

Ephraim said that the same gas station was actually abandoned on that Black Sabbath due to the multiple alarms and the terrorists' break-in, so the soldiers came to this store and began to operate it.

"Popsicles, cigarettes, soft drinks, coffee, phone chargers, and the soldiers distributed essential products for free to the security forces, ZAKA and MDA volunteers, and anyone who needed them following the attacks. The soldiers took the initiative and provided the service themselves. The IDF managed the gas station," he said.

When I tried to find out where the owners were, he told me that it was probably a Bedouin who managed to escape and that he was still trying to find out the details of the incident.

Ephraim also shared an unusual event that made me very angry.

He did hope not to talk about it, but I asked for details.

"There were a lot of bodies on Route 232, even after Saturday. I took the initiative to evacuate those bodies, hoping that the IDF soldiers would not see them as it would hurt their morale. I took it upon myself," he said.

While Ephraim managed to secure dozens of volunteers and ambulances, he was able to secure only one refrigerated truck for the mission. When he turned to the Israeli Police requesting more refrigerated trucks, he encountered a bureaucracy that did not match the actual situation.

"They transferred me from one department to another. The police transport company told me that they needed a policeman to approve the truck order. The police have refrigerated trucks, which are supposed to be used exactly for this type of case, but because I couldn't find a policeman to give permission, I could not get the trucks."

"Do you understand that this is a system failure?" I asked Ephraim, who was not convinced.

"You cannot blame anyone. There are no guilty parties in this event of the Black Sabbath. It is a chain of mishaps that someone beyond our control caused. We cannot understand it. Even if you try, you will not get answers - one big fog. And yet, I came out of this event with more faith." Ephraim admittedly came out with more faith, but he will not forget the horrors he witnessed on the roads of hell, in the 'Migniot[5], 'in the moshavim[6] and the kibbutzim.

---

5. A portable protection unit ("migunit") – a non-standard protected space, a portable unit made as one piece of reinforced concrete (or a material with similar properties).
6. A type of Israeli village/town or Jewish community, in particular a type of cooperative agricultural community of individual farms.

"We brought out huge carts with about twenty bodies each. The condition of the bodies was appalling. They were burned, and some of them hugged each other. Some of them were joined so that they could not be distinguished. We opened a carpet on the floor and tried to figure out who was who and which bag to put him in when it was actually one big lump. You're afraid to put two people in the same bag, but you can't tell them apart; it's one lump."

In order to better understand, I asked him, "Why was it so difficult to identify the bodies?"

His answer will shock every human being.

"I couldn't tell the difference between a head, a leg, a hand. I couldn't tell if the part of the body I was looking at belonged to the body next to it. What we did was take all the body parts of the various limbs off the carts and place them on a large carpet that we spread on the floor, and we tried to figure out which part belonged to whom. Which corpse was two corpses, and which corpse was half a corpse, and whose parts needed to be connected somehow to be put in the same bag? Some were without legs, some without arms, some without internal organs, some completely burned, stuck together. I didn't know if the severed head belonged to the teeth that were next to it or if they belonged to someone else whose leg was cut off."

He continued his testimony, "You try to decipher it. You see two skulls that are connected to each other and one body. You understand that it is two people. But where is the body of the other person? And which of the skulls does the body in front of us now belong to? So, you try to separate the skulls to try to identify them. Do you think you should put them in one bag or two separate bags so that they understand that these are two bodies?

These things are essential because if you decide to put an unidentified body part such as a certain organ, a hand, a leg, fingers or a skull into the same bag with another body, a situation of mass graves may arise, or a situation in which a certain family will not have a grave to cry over."

Indeed, as Ephraim described, one can only imagine his and his friends' work as a giant puzzle that needs to be solved. The puzzle's various parts are unrecognizable, and it's not even clear if the pieces in front of you belong to the puzzle you're trying to put together or to another puzzle.

Usually, we complain that we get confused between the similar parts of a puzzle. The ones that always make it difficult for us to solve it, like the sky, the grass, or the water, whose parts look almost the same. The next time you sit down with your little one and solve a puzzle, try to imagine what parts the ZAKA workers tried to put together. Were those parts teeth, legs, hands, arms, and skulls? Or intestines, kidneys, fingers, eyes, and breasts? And no, they didn't complain about the difficulty.

Ephraim described the horror he witnessed in his own words in a poem titled "The Corpses That Smiled At Us."

"No matter what you look like, if you look at all,
It doesn't matter if you smell like dirt and ashes,
The smell around you - it doesn't matter to us at all,
We came to take you!!!
And you who are silent on the earth,
You understand very well who we are,
And what is our role in all this chaos,
and the mute language of the blind/deaf/toddlers and amputees,
without words, in a language that only we understand,
And with a winning smile on your face or your still body,

Such smiles that only we can see.
Heroic smiles of kibbutzniks and passers-by,
Heroic smiles of policemen and policewomen, soldiers and female soldiers,
Heroic smiles of leftists and rightists, religious and non-religious male and female celebrants,
heroic smiles of infants that have not tasted sin,
heroic smiles of curly and non-curly-haired children,
heroic smiles of girls with long hair or short ponytails,
Heroic smiles of children with parents next to them and without parents next to them.
Heroic smiles of those who were there.
Yes, you ZAKA volunteers,
Yes, you. The ones who are wearing the yellow vests that we know from the bombing attacks,
We expected you for hours and days, but we knew,
We knew you would come in the end, and here you are!!!
and we have not yet answered,
You continue with a welcoming smile and say:
Before you start with your holy work, please look around you.
Look and understand what really happened here for twelve, twenty-four and even seventy-two hours straight.
Your request - our request, your commandment - our commandment, and honoring the dead is our motto.
We stop for a moment and look. Left, right and left again,
Like a small child about to cross a busy road with trepidation.
We feel the last minutes and hours of the bodies smiling at us,
War and holocaust heroes, childhood heroes and horror movies,
Heroes like ten royals slain who suffered and rose in sanctity and storm.
You, heroes, stay a moment,
then continue and command us a holy transaction as holy heroes for sacred people:

You ZAKA people, tell everyone, tell the world!
And as much as possible in preserving our last dignity,
that everything that is said and described about the actions of those
miscreants is true,
Holy heroes, we went, and we fought until the last moment!!!
We give our consent, and a holy transaction is closed in silence.
Among heroes and saints for ZAKA volunteers.
And now, when you are already relaxed, your smile has faded.
As a kind of consent to the continuation of our holy work, to which
we have come.
Your holy and martyred body, big or small,
is then placed by us in holy fear into the holy bag of ZAKA
to your last way.
We will not forget to keep the words of the dead,
But we will also never forget the smiles of those heroes at that time:
A smile that said it all without words,
Smile of the bodies of saints and heroes,
A smile of hidden righteous people that only ZAKA volunteers get
to see,
A smile that gave us the strength to move on to the next saint,
A smile that gave us the strength to return to ourselves and our
family in peace."

"At the request of the family member, we kept digging and went over every piece of land. The person does not exist; there is no trace left of him. This was the condition of most of the bodies on the roads of hell."

"Route 232 is the main axis of the communities surrounding Gaza, a strategic route with security significance," the Israel Routes website wrote back in 2020. They added, "Before the upgrade, this road was defined as a bloody road where many fatal accidents occurred." Indeed, Israel Routes Company upgraded the road at a cost of no less than one hundred and ninety-four million shekels. One of the three main goals of the upgrade, which, as mentioned, cost quite a bit, was "providing a response to the vehicles of the rescue forces and the security forces during a security emergency."

"Only in retrospect do you realize that you were saved by a miracle. You realize that the same bypass road, 232, which goes all the way to Kerem Shalom, was filled with live terrorists while we were working on clearing it," Ephraim told me. "There were IDF tanks surrounding it as if we were in Jenin."

Route 34, which starts at the Nativot junction and ends at the Yad Mordechai junction, also suffered the inferno of the Black Sabbath.

"Until we were told that the road was full of bodies, we didn't understand why we couldn't enter there. When we entered the road, we began to understand the scale of the event that was taking place. There were burned vehicles and bodies everywhere, and this was twelve hours from the beginning of the event. Everything was a mess; there was no order for the IDF vehicles that wanted to advance on the road, but there were bodies on it. We, as ZAKA, wanted to evacuate bodies - but we had to allow the security forces to move. There was complete chaos," Ephraim said. "Then we drove on Route 232 to get to the party in Re'im. The road was Sodom and Gomorrah. I can't even explain it to you."

When I asked him to try explaining anyway, he asked me if I had been to Hollywood.

"In Hollywood, they show you how they produce an action movie: with smoke, fire, cars flying through the air, ones that overturn have fire, noise and debris come out of them. On Route 232, I felt like I was witnessing something that was ten times worse than what I saw in Hollywood. I drove in zigzags so I wouldn't run over the bodies and saw cars dumped, upside down, burned. This was not a specific section of the road but the entire length of the road. Everywhere, in the middle and on the sides. I drove and managed to avoid dozens of bodies. In retrospect, I understand that the road was still filled with terrorists. How did we survive? I really don't know."

Simcha also witnessed the horrors on the roads.

"I arrived with the truck at Junction 34, turning left towards Be'eri onto Highway 232, and I saw upside down and burnt cars. At that moment, I was sure it was an unreported rocket hit or an unintentional accident. When we got out of the big truck, we saw bodies and wanted to start treating them, but the large amount of dead people aroused suspicion. We started receiving reports that we were near live terrorists and that we had to leave the place immediately."

Even for Simcha, working on the road was not easy.

"When we arrived at the Shaar HaNegev intersection, already on Route 34 at the entrance to Sderot, I looked and saw a pile of about twenty bodies. We drove on this road in a slalom between burnt cars and corpses and live terrorists from whom we had to flee. A four-minute drive from the 34/232 intersection to Shaar HaNegev took no less than four and a half hours. Every time we saw a vehicle, we stopped and loaded the bodies. Just from the road, I had thirty-eight bodies, which included everyone - soldiers, civilians, policemen, everyone."

The story was continued by Reuven, who also told about the road massacre.

"We arrived in the Sderot area and began to collect all the bodies that were on the road. In all my life, not even while volunteering for ZAKA, I have never seen so many bodies in one place."

Reuven verified and repeated his friend Simcha's story that at the entrance to Sderot, in the middle of the square, they collected twenty corpses grouped together in a pile. These are the first twenty corpses collected and grouped from the roads of hell.

"Then I continued to Road 232, and I just collected and wrapped all the bodies that were on the way. Bodies of civilians who simply escaped from every possible place and were killed along the way by shooting and grenades. They (the terrorists) didn't care who it was. Children and elderly people were there. They also confirmed every killing. I know that sounds delusional, a joke, or an invention. But in every yard, in each yard where we drove, there was a body. It was the Wild West."

Reuven also said that the road trip, which should take no more than a few minutes, took many hours.

Jamal told how, on the way to Sderot, he saw an Israeli motorcyclist lying on the road.

He approached him to find out what happened and noticed that he had been shot in the head. When he raised his head to look around, he saw a large number of old men shot on the floor.

"I advanced towards Kfar Aza and saw a group of IDF soldiers on the road. I started to approach them to see if they needed any assistance. As soon as I got close, they stood in shooting range and started shooting in my direction. It turns out that they were actually terrorists dressed as soldiers who tried to mislead us. Miraculously, we managed to escape," he said. "From there, I continued to Road 232, and all around me, I saw dead bodies. During the whole drive, I only saw bodies thrown on the road. I didn't know how to react," Jamal said with incredible difficulty.

We have already heard Ephraim's testimony regarding the infernal roads, but Shlomo, who was assigned to work with him on the roads, told me about their humorous relationship and how it was used as a way to cope with this terrible situation. He also told me how he read the situation.

"I saw abandoned vehicles on the sides of the road, and I wondered, like Ephraim, what happened? Is this a woman who was frightened by the missile? Ephraim told me that I was delusional and ordered me to 'wake up and smell the coffee,'" said Shlomo.

Each testimony aligns with the next one, as Shlomo said that Ephraim shared with him, in those very moments, the same comparison that I myself received from him about Hollywood and action movies.

"He told me that they made an action movie with shooting and everything. Only that the movie was real."

He also shared what he experienced on the roads personally.

"Everywhere there were corpses and abandoned and burned vehicles. I saw that there were so many corpses and that we were filling the trucks to the brim. I had a hard time with this because we usually don't do this and respect the dead, but I realized that this time, there was no choice. One of the most chilling cases I had

Alon Penzel

while I was on the road was when I came to one particular body. Because it was burned, it was impossible to tell if it was a man or a woman. It was burnt to the core. But the real problem was that the body's arms were spread to the side in such a way that we couldn't put the body in the bag. I had no choice but to break the arms and pin them to the body. There was no other option, especially since the body was burned and there were no tissues at all."

Natan completed the chilling testimony about the roads of hell.

"I entered Road 232 and asked myself if I was in the State of Israel. When I entered the road, I did not understand the magnitude of the horror."

I asked Natan what he saw on the road.

"I was exposed to a war scene. To the right side and the left side, either burned, charred, shot, or dismantled, I slowly began to understand that these were vehicles that had people in them. I started seeing bodies. The bodies were in a horrifying condition, with tiny pieces remaining. In some places, there was nothing left."

Natan shared a personal story that touched him, and, like many others, it happened on the roads of death.

"Two weeks after the Black Sabbath, I got a call from a random guy. He told me he was in a car with his brother at the Sdot Negev intersection during the inferno."

The same guy who called Natan was indeed injured but managed to escape, leaving his brother, who was murdered, in the car.

"My brother was murdered, but he is still listed as missing because no part of his body can be found. Please come and help me find his remains so I can bury him," the man pleaded with Natan.

Natan said that he reached the location with his team to help the man with his painful request. "We kept digging and went over every piece of land - he doesn't exist," he said painfully. "We got some things out of there, but I highly doubt they will be able to extract DNA from them."

At my request, Natan told me how vehicles and the people inside them were in a state where nothing was left of them. "The car's fuel tank catching fire was just the beginning. The terrorists didn't stop there; they kept burning the car to ensure nothing was left. The heat was so intense that even the iron in the tires melted, turning to liquid. They wanted to eliminate any trace of the person who had been inside the car."

On the Israel Routes website, it is written that Route 232 has an indisputable security significance, and we are exposed to this fact in a clear and cruel way in the testimonies of October 7th. Indeed, it is ironic that this road was already defined many years ago as a bloody road due to the number of fatal accidents that occurred on it and will forever be immortalized as such, except that nothing that happened on that Black Sabbath was an accident. As for the question of whether the expensive upgrade of the Israel Routes company was indeed successful in "providing a response to the vehicles of the rescue units during a security emergency," according to them, the State of Israel will have to provide answers to its citizens, this amidst the fog that prevails over hundreds of similar questions concerning the greatest failure our country has ever known.

Alon Penzel

"There are no cats in Be'eri."

"On the first night, we focused on collecting the bodies at the party in Re'im.

The pressure was very high because the number of bodies was huge, and we had a limited time to evacuate them due to the security situation," Reuven told me. "Among all the madness, we found an injured dog, and I couldn't leave it there. I put it in the car, and in the morning, we took it to the vet, who also managed to find its owner, a family that escaped from Kibbutz Be'eri."

I asked Reuven to share more cases involving animals with me.

"We entered one of the apartments in one of the kibbutzim and found the body of an elderly woman, surrounded by her seven cats - all murdered," Reuven said that all the cats, as well as the elderly woman, were shot dead.

Shlomo also talked about Hamas's cruelty towards animals.

"In the second house I entered in Be'eri, I saw a woman hugging a dog. Both were murdered. It seems that she was trying to protect the dog so that the murderers would not kill it. There is no reason for a dog on the street to be killed. A dog also has its right to exist, and they denied him the right to exist in the world. Why? The devil knows why."

Natan said, "A bright spot for me was that a few days after I saw a terrorist shoot a dog to death, I was exposed to a picture of the same terrorist lying next to the dog." He added, "In general, they tried to slaughter everything that passed in front of them even the animals. I can tell you something hard and painful, probably unimaginable, but this is the reality: there are no cats in Be'eri. More so, there is no living thing in Be'eri. You can't even hear birds chirping."

I found it difficult to imagine the situation that Natan described to me, in which not even one animal in the kibbutz survived.

"They just shot the cats that were in the street?" I asked.

He answered me simply, "There is nothing left of the animals."

And we can only wonder what those animals did to the Hamas terrorists. What was their crime? Why were they murdered in cold blood? What was their great sin, since they did not even hold Israeli citizenship, nor were they even Jews? They never had an opinion about the Israeli-Palestinian conflict, the existence of which they were not even aware.

Those animals did not know who Israel was or who Hamas was. They never chose a side in the war for this land. They simply loved humans, but did not realize that the people they encountered on October 7th were not humans at all.

"A pile of seventy seven bodies in one packed truck. We piled them one on top of the other in bags. There was no room for anything. Yes, there was confusion between the bodies of victims and the bodies of terrorists."

"On October 7th, on that Black Sabbath, I retrieved twenty bodies from the party in Re'im, which were added to thirty-eight bodies from Highway 34 and another twenty bodies from Sderot and Highway 232," Simcha told me. "My truck was packed from the floor to the ceiling with seventy-two bodies. We squeezed them into a pile, one on top of the other. It was crazy! The truck was packed."

When I asked Simcha what the average number of bodies usually put in a ZAKA truck is, I was amazed at the answer.

"In an extreme emergency, the maximum number of bodies I've placed in a truck was fourteen. When Command asked me who the bodies in my truck belonged to, I could only answer that it was a 'mixture' including soldiers, policemen, civilians, terrorists, every-thing," he shared.

While Simcha was telling me about his truck, I could only share with him what was going through my mind at those moments - gas trucks or horrifyingly packed trains during World War II, when Jews were squeezed to death in those vehicles on their way to be exterminated.

I asked him to detail the division of the bodies and their insertion into the bags, wondering how it would be possible to distinguish, afterward, between the bodies of civilians and the bodies of terror-ists, especially during wartime.

Simcha replied, "We marked each bag before we closed it. We put soldiers in specific IDF bags, and the police also had their own special bags. We put the terrorists in bags, turned them over and wrote in giant letters - 'terrorist.'"

I tried to find out how ZAKA volunteers agreed to also evacuate terrorist bodies after the horrors they witnessed.

I got the answer from Reuven, "The only reason we were willing to undertake the mission, at the request of the state, to collect the bodies of the terrorists was the knowledge that it might save the lives of kidnapped Israelis in any potential deal in the future. Some volunteers did not agree to evacuate the bodies of the terrorists, and our mission was to explain to those volunteers the importance of the matter and that it would be in the best interest of the people of Israel. The operational rank of the IDF also tried explaining this to the volunteers. We realized that to secure the release of all our hostages in Gaza, we would need to offer something in exchange, and that is why we agreed. We did it with a heavy heart. In the white bags, we put the Jews, the holy ones, and in the black bags, we put the terrorists to distinguish between the impure and the pure."

"Where are the bodies of the terrorists now?" I asked Reuven, who replied, "They are in Israeli territory, in refrigeration. We refrigerated them for future negotiation. I hope that in the end, all the filth we collected will pay off."

He also talked about seeing the packed trucks for the first time in his life and how he tried to cope with the load.

"I was responsible for arranging the bodies at the party in Re'im that evening. Thanks to the experience I gained with the trucks in

Meron[7] , my role was to arrange them in the various trucks. I sat and counted each body that entered the truck. It was an insane amount. In Meron, I loaded about fifteen bodies into a truck. This time, I had to calculate how to arrange the bodies in advance. In one truck, there were fifty-five bodies and in another, seventy-seven. In trucks that typically carried ten bodies, I managed to fit thirty-three. I developed a neat formula for stacking the bodies, and I knew how I wanted them to look in the end."

I also asked Reuven to explain the division of the bodies into victims and terrorists.

"In one truck, there were only soldiers, another truck with only civilians and as mentioned, we also had to collect those disgusting people from there. Unfortunately, we gave the terrorists a separate truck, which they didn't deserve at all. I would have tied them with a rope and dragged them as far as necessary."

I tried to find out from Simcha and Reuven if, despite the clear division according to the colors of bags, separate trucks and labeling, there were still identification errors between victims and terrorists.

Reuven replied, "At the party itself, there were almost no mistakes because most of the civilians there were not armed. So, anyone who had a weapon next to him was a terrorist, and if not, then you could see that it was a soldier or a policeman. You can see that it was someone different from those stinking disgusting villains."

On the other hand, Simcha said that despite the efforts, there were still identification errors.

---

7. An incident that happened on April 2021: a deadly crowd crush occurred on Mount Meron during the annual pilgrimage to the tomb of Rabbi Shimon bar Yochai on the Jewish holiday of Lag BaOmer.

"With all that, over time, the areas came under the military control of the Home Front Command, so ZAKA could no longer identify each and every person meticulously as we did at the beginning by putting special stickers and associating the body with the right truck. We just loaded and moved on as fast as possible." Simcha said, "There were many bodies that were tagged as terrorists and in the end, after a DNA test, they realized that they were civilians."

"While I was in command, I insisted that if we did not know for sure whether it was a civilian body or a terrorist body, we should put the bag upside down (as is customary for terrorist bodies) but add a giant question mark five times on the bag so they know there is a doubt," he said.

When I asked Simcha if such mistakes actually happened, he nodded.

"It also happened in Alumim, where Thai civilians were brutally murdered and butchered, and there were identification errors between them and the terrorists."

Reuven, who is also responsible for logistics equipment at ZAKA, summed up, "I collected from ZAKA warehouses all the helmets, body armor, body bags, and other ZAKA equipment. I had to take so much from there. I emptied a quarter of a warehouse in one second. I've already been in mass events in Meron and managed the entire logistics system, but this time, it was shocking because we were also under hellfire."

Reuven said that when he began to understand the number of bodies involved, he immediately called the command.

"I told them, do you remember the event in Meron? At those moments, I told you how many trucks were needed. Here, we need many more trucks. When the command asked me if it was really that extreme, I could only reply, yes." This conversation was burned into Reuven's mind, who said, "It was a conversation about corpses, not people."

Natan shared the equipment issue from a different perspective, from the side of the IDF soldiers.

"As soon as we entered Kfar Aza and the soldiers saw an Israeli rescue vehicle, they immediately asked us if we had any medical equipment. From the moment we answered yes, not a few minutes passed, and we didn't have any equipment left. It turned out that the forces in the field had no medical equipment left either. Nothing. They needed equipment so urgently that they didn't leave even a band-aid in our bags."

As I described during this testimony, the imagination of a human being, especially a Jew and third-generation Holocaust survivor who visited the extermination camps in Europe, immediately made me think of the Holocaust when faced with this scenario. The trucks filled to the brim, and the ambulances that drove the bodies were, in my head, just another version of the death trains.

The question arises: how is it possible that the Jewish people went through their second holocaust, or in more subtle terminology, an unimaginable disaster precisely when they had a sovereign and independent state with one of the strongest armies in the world?

The State of Israel will have to give answers to this crucial question, both to its living citizens and to those who are no longer with us, and it would do well to provide them soon.

"Only in Yad Vashem can one see such a quantity of corpses as at the Re'im festival. And the amount of blood? Not something that can even be described."

"There's nothing you can do with them. They just wanted to dance[8]." These song lyrics best describe the people who partied at the Nova festival, the nature raves near Re'im.

At least three hundred and forty-seven civilians and seventeen policemen were brutally murdered while they just wanted to dance, celebrate, and hang out. They were boys, young people, adults, and even elderly people whose only sin was the desire to bring more joy, laughter, love, and creation into the world - pure happiness.

Those who prevented it were those who did everything in their power to introduce burning hatred and unimaginable evil into the world.

This is how the ZAKA volunteers experienced the nightmare.

"At the beginning, we collected the bodies based on the identification of their name, as in any scene of a murder or an incident of unnatural death. Accurate numbering and taking fingerprints from the body is a regular process. But between 1:00 a.m. and 2:00 a.m. on the night between October 7th and 8th, i.e., between the Black Sabbath and Sunday, reports began to arrive that at 4:00 a.m., at the crack of dawn, there were expected to be more terrorist infiltrations into Israeli territory. We needed to make sure that by then, there wouldn't be a single body left at the scene," Natan told me.

---

8. Lyrics from an Israeli song by Moshe Peretz and Omer Adam.

In every testimony I've heard, the order given to ZAKA volunteers, rescue, and security forces was mentioned.

This order, apparently issued by the IDF General Commander, was based on intelligence information predicting that at 4:00 a.m. on Sunday, October 8th, there would be additional terrorist infiltrations into Israeli territory alongside another missile attack. To protect the security forces and ensure the collection of the bodies, ZAKA volunteers faced an almost impossible task: to gather hundreds of charred and dismembered bodies in only a few hours.

"In order to meet the goal, we started packing without documentation. We started transferring the bodies from the party area to a checkpoint, and at that point, we simply put the bodies in bags and sent them to the trucks so that at 3:50 a.m., the area was free of bodies," Natan shared.

When I asked Natan about the condition of the bodies he found at the party, he told me that due to the speed at which they worked to collect all the bodies, he was busy primarily packing and didn't really have time to look at the condition of the bodies in front of him. He predicted that ninety-eight percent of the victims were shot in the face, and all of them had confirmed kills. This means that the terrorists shot them all again to ensure their deaths.

But Natan was not the only volunteer at the party.

Ephraim, who arrived before him, had time to see the horrors.

"We entered the party area. We still saw the lights, the Coca-Cola refrigerators, bars - and an insane number of bodies. If you want to imagine the amount in your head, the only thing you can think of that will describe it properly is the Holocaust. Only in Yad Vashem will you see such a large number of corpses. We collected corpses, but it did not end. We finished one area and moved to another. I did not understand where I was or what happened there, and there was not much time to think either. The amount of blood that was there is not something I can even describe properly."

Ephraim continued; this time, he shared his opinion of what happened at the party.

"In my opinion, the terrorists did not know about the party. Although many people claim that they did, from what I have seen and heard, they did not know. Relative to the number of participants in the party and considering the number of terrorists that we saw arrive at the party compared to other places like Kfar Aza and Be'eri, there were not enough bodies of civilians and terrorists. I mean, if they had known about the party, there would not have been three hundred dead but two thousand, and they would have concentrated all their forces on the party. I believe that they encountered a party 'on the way' because if they had known about a group of over three thousand people together, as was the case at the party, they would not have gone to the communities, the kibbutzim at all, they would not have concentrated in other places. They would have only gone to the party. So, it's clear to me they had no information about the party."

"After we finished working on the roads, the crew was eager to get to the party area," Shlomo told me. "When I was told 'the party area,' I still imagined loud music, dancing, revelers, and strong drinks. Otherwise, what else could be at a party?"

Shlomo emphasized how, in retrospect, there was no understanding of the magnitude of the event, even when the evening of that Black Sabbath had already arrived.

His friend from the ZAKA organization, Reuven, testified that the number of bodies that came from the party was so great that the ZAKA trucks were filled to the brim.

"Full of bodies in a state I've never seen; there was a body everywhere you looked. The party is probably the only place where there was nobody without a bullet in the head; it simply did not exist. Everyone who was murdered received a bullet in the head to ensure a kill. Everyone, including everyone," said Jamal.

While the extent of the disaster is becoming clear, we can only ask ourselves how a party that celebrated peace turned into an unprecedented bloodbath, whether the Hamas terrorists knew of its existence or not. Since it is not my personal role to investigate the incident, all I could do was imagine myself at that party at those moments and wonder how I would have reacted and how I would have acted.

Would I come to the aid of my friends, or would I run for my life?

Would I get out of there alive and injured, maybe kidnapped, maybe manage to escape unscathed?

The answers to the questions were vague. My heart was beating fast, and my thoughts continued to run nonstop inside my brain.

Sometimes, it seemed that I would never find answers, which really frustrated me. Then I understood, made peace, and came to terms with the fact that many did find answers.

The difference between me and them is that most of them are now in heaven.

"They gouged out the eye of the family's father. The mother's breast was cut off. The little girl's foot was amputated, and the seven year old boy's fingers were cut off. While the family was bleeding to death, the terrorists set up a table in front of them and started eating."

Between each testimony, I wondered if evil has limits. That is, would even the cruelest people on earth refrain from doing certain unimaginable things that they see as a red line that should not be crossed?

The answer to this question slowly became clear to me as I was exposed to the stories of the October 7th horrors.

Sometimes, when I listened to those horrors, like the one you will be exposed to in the upcoming testimony, I felt as if I was watching one of the terrifying 'Saw' movies. But then I realized that if the writers of 'Saw' had chosen to write such a script, it would have been rejected immediately due to lack of credibility.

This time, I asked Jamal to focus on the brutality of the terrorists from a different angle, and this is what he had to say, "When we entered the houses, there was not a single house where the Hamas terrorists didn't have a meal. They just set up tables and ate. You ask yourself if they ate before they murdered the people or after the murders. As soon as you discover that in all the houses, the refrigerators were opened and all the food was on the tables, everything was eaten and drunk, you understand that the families did not eat before the incident, but terrorists." I just kept thinking to myself how a human being could eat while watching others bleed to death. But then again, very quickly, the realization came back that these are not human beings at all.

Natan also shared more about the "appetite" of the Hamas terrorists.

"When I entered the first home in Kibbutz Be'eri, I found a man who had apparently prepared a holiday meal for him and his family. Not only did the family not get to enjoy that meal, but I understood that while the terrorists unimaginably abused that family, they sat and ate the meal in their place, in front of them, while the family bled to death." Natan explained to me that this could be deduced from the connection between the time of the murders and the scene. "People don't eat holiday dinner at six in the morning," he told me painfully.

Yossi also witnessed the brutality of those terrorists.

"In Be'eri, we witnessed a family that was subjected to unimaginable abuse. The terrorists sat and ate while they gouged out one of the father's eyes while his hands were handcuffed behind his back. The mother of that family also had her hands handcuffed behind her back, and they removed her breasts. They simply cut it. So, the father had an eye hanging out, and the mother was bleeding out from her breast. All this happened in front of their little children, who were sitting in front of them."

If you thought that was enough for the terrorists, think again because the horrors did not end there.

"The terrorists cut off several fingers from the seven-year-old boy's hands right in front of his parent's eyes. They also 'took care' of the daughter and cut off her leg," Yossi said.

Yossi also said that the terrorists set up a table in the middle of the house, in front of those four unfortunate souls who were bleeding to death, whose lives were ended most cruelly and started eating.

And we can only imagine in our heads the sights, and perhaps also the feelings, of the father and mother of the family before they were murdered, watching helplessly as their children were butchered right in front of them.

Try to imagine the helplessness that the father and mother experienced in those moments. Not only could they not do anything to prevent their children from experiencing what they experienced, but they also had to be there for them while they themselves were dealing with a gouged eye and a cut-off breast.

Many other disturbing and sadistic questions persist, haunting the mind relentlessly:

Was the last sight of the father before his eye was taken out of the abuse his wife and children endured?

And what about those little children? Those children who did not hurt anyone, witnessed the cruel abuse of their parents, and then experienced it themselves? What were the family members' last words to each other, if there were even any?

I returned to my question at the beginning of this testimony, a question whose answer I personally have already deciphered, "Does evil have limits?"

This time, I will make an exception and let you come to your own conclusions.

"They took a nail gun and nailed the guy to the door. They stuck nail after nail into his body and crucified him vertically."

"ZAKA is usually not active on Saturday unless there is an international event such as the one on October 7th," Natan told me. "I was observing the Shabbat, and it was also 'Simhat Torah,' and the organization's radio started working abnormally. At first, it sounded like another shooting event at the South and the Center, but we didn't attach any real importance to it. I don't know how to explain the complacency of the security forces and my own complacency," he said.

Natan said that the synagogue he goes to on Saturday mornings has at least twenty medics, paramedics, security personnel and rescue forces. Their lack of understanding of the magnitude of the event was so significant that none of them thought about opening their phones and checking what happened.

"At those moments, we were looking at the sky, that is the rockets. We thought that it was indeed a more massive attack than usual because the devices still beeped, but we did not imagine what was happening on the ground."

Natan said that as soon as he began to understand how serious the situation was, he immediately took the car and drove towards Re'im.

"The work at the party and on the roads was very intense. We collected human parts and what was left of people from the roads, from the cars, from hundreds of different scenes. It was not easy, but it was just the first part."

I immediately asked him about the "second part."

"Was there any stage in the days after the attack, or until now actually, that you arrived at one of the kibbutzim or the communities of Be'eri, Kfar Aza, Nahal Oz, Sderot, Ofakim and took care of the people who were murdered in their homes or on the streets of the kibbutz?"

Natan immediately replied, "Until Monday morning, I saw people who had been murdered, but I was mostly busy packing the bodies. But that Monday morning, when I got to Be'eri, everything turned upside down for me." Natan stopped for a few seconds.

"Tell me the details," I asked him with slight trepidation.

"The sights were different, and the scenes were different. The horrors and abuse were unimaginable. They committed Mengele's atrocities[9] on the residents," he answered.

"Is this something you feel you can or are able to tell me? Share with me?" I asked.

The room was silent for almost half a minute. No one spoke. Natan hesitated for a while, thinking about what he wanted to say.

"There were nasty scenes in the houses. In one of the houses, an old man kept a nail gun in the house. They pierced him all over his body."

I insisted that he tell me the exact details of the event, and after pondering my request, Natan decided to share.

"When we entered the house, we were shocked. You see a dead body in front of you, and you can't digest the way that dead body

---

9. Josef Mengele - "The Angel of Death" (German: Todesengel), he performed deadly experiments on prisoners at the Auschwitz II (Birkenau) concentration camp, where he was a member of the team of doctors who selected victims to be murdered in the gas chambers and was one of the doctors who administered the gas.

looks, the way we found it. At first glance, we didn't see the nail gun. We saw the human being."

Once again, I urged Natan to tell me more details about the form in which the body was found so that I would fully understand the situation. I admit that despite all the evidence I have been exposed to so far, I did not expect this answer.

But just before he gave me that horrible answer, Natan received a real-time call on the ZAKA radio.

"Bialik Street in Tel Aviv, it's an HDA[10] incident." He asked me if I knew what HDA was, and before I could answer him that yes, I did, the walkie-talkie continued to work: "There is an active shooting inside a restaurant."

We waited anxiously to understand what was happening, but the radio remained silent.

"This silence is the worst. We may have to cut it short," he told me. One moment before we ended the interview, a report was received on the walkie-talkie that the event had ended, and Natan and I continued our conversation.

"Then we entered the house," he continued his testimony, "and we simply saw a human body standing. His head was slumped, and the body was pinned to the door frame. We didn't understand what we were seeing at all. Then, we noticed a nail gun on the floor, which apparently belonged to that resident. The terrorists nailed him to the door frame. Yes, they nailed him to the door frame. It was one of the craziest things we ever saw."

I asked Natan which door they nailed him to, and he replied, "Not at the entrance to the house. Inside the house. We went inside, and

---

10. Hostile Destructive Activity (military).

for a moment, we didn't understand how the man was standing because he was dead. This is what I say all the time: they were busy abusing people."

With a slight stutter for fear of continuing the testimony, I asked, "What do you mean by 'nailed him'? His feet were on the floor?"

Natan raised his voice a little, "It was a strange sight. He was barely standing, and his head fell forward. He was nailed to the door frame. Of course, he also had a bullet in his head."

I asked Natan if his crucifixion was, in fact, done before or after he was murdered, and Natan said he had no way of knowing.

"I'm not one of those people who watches sadistic movies, but let's just say that if they had working tools in every house, then it would have been worse. They abused women, children, babies, old people, everything that came along," he said.

Even though I already understood precisely what had happened, that the guy was actually crucified, I probably wasn't able to comprehend how such a thing could be done to a human being standing in front of you. Again, with horrifying innocence, I asked Natan, "Please explain it to me. Where do you have to stab a person to nail him into a door frame?"

At that moment, Natan sighed and raised his voice a little, not as someone who was angry but as someone who sympathized with the innocence that he no longer had since October 7th.

"Do you know what a construction nail looks like?" he asked while using his hands to show me the enormous size of the nail. "So yes, nails this size were inserted into his body parts. With these nails they stuck his body into the crossbar in rows. Nail after nail. It was a crucifixion, only here they nailed him to the crossbar vertically," he described.

I could only sympathize with what Natan told me during the conversation when he compared those atrocities with Mengele's atrocities. But when I expressed that solidarity, Natan added, "I will tell you something more than that. Mengele also did medical research. They didn't do any research. Supposably, Mengele can argue that his ideology is that the Jews are parasites, that he does research on mice, and that the Jews are his mice. But in this case, it wasn't research. It was abuse, so you know what? They're worse than Mengele."

"They inserted metal wires through their stomachs into their bodies and tied them together. Both were naked."

"I arrived at the gas station near Kibbutz Kfar Aza. It was a sort of meeting point for ZAKA volunteers in those days," Natan told me. "There, we received a truck with the bodies of Thai citizens who had been butchered in the field. We loaded them into our truck and were about to leave. Just before I started the engine, two soldiers grabbed me and just threw me into the back of a tractor before crazy shooting started from all directions."

It turned out, according to him, that the IDF soldiers received information on the ground in real-time about three or four terrorists that were nearby, next to the gas station.

"They threw me into the backhoe loader so I wouldn't get hurt. For many minutes, there was crazy shooting until the soldiers managed to eliminate the terrorists," said Natan, who survived the encounter.

The live shooting, the constant fear, the danger and working in a war zone (something he and his friends were not used to) was the easy part for the volunteers, who had to witness unimaginable horrors in the various kibbutzim.

"We arrived at the kibbutz once again on Wednesday morning. This day is engraved in my memory and will remain with me forever. Several days had already passed since the attack, and there was already a smell at this point. The terrible sights combined with other senses made the experience even more difficult. The most horrific situation I encountered," he continued, "was when we entered one of the destroyed houses in the kibbutz after receiving a call about an extremely pungent smell from the place. We entered the house by climbing over the ruins because they were completely destroyed. Suddenly, we saw a mattress and a girl tied to it. We tried to separate her from the mattress, but we couldn't and didn't understand why. When we looked closer, we noticed that metal wires were running inside her body. We were sure these were threads from the mattress that entered her body. Therefore, we began to clear the rubble that was around the mattress. What we saw under the rubble was unbelievable."

Natan took a deep breath and continued his testimony, "So we moved the rubble and the mattress, but we could not separate her from it. Suddenly, we realized that the girl was actually tied to a man, apparently her partner on the other side of the mattress. Both were completely naked."

So many questions came to my mind, but Natan didn't stop, "I couldn't really understand what was in front of me. They weren't shot. I didn't see a shot wound, so I don't know what was done to them and with them."

"Explain to me what does that mean. Did they put metal wires into their stomachs? into their bodies?" I asked him.

He replied, "Yes, they inserted metal wires into their bodies through their stomachs and tied them together on both sides of the mattress."

I insisted that he tell me more about the case.

"I'm sorry to ask these questions and go into depth, but it's my duty. Can you describe to me exactly how it happened? Did they insert the wires on both sides of their stomachs? How do you actually do something like that?"

Natan didn't like the question at all. He didn't want to repeat the painful things, yet he made an effort for the testimony, "As I've said, metal wires were inserted through their bodies. Whole metal wires were inserted through the stomach. From both sides to the both of them, so that they would be tied together on both sides of the mattress." He concluded, "It was horrifying. That coldness. You can't contain it."

And again, we are left with unanswered questions.

Did that couple end their lives after losing so much blood due to the wires that were inserted into their bodies? Did they endure other atrocities that were committed against them? After all, both were found utterly naked on both sides of the mattress. And how did all this happen in real-time? Did the couple look at each other, maybe even whisper their last words? Did they at least, as if there is any consolation in that, die together as one body connected to each other so that it seemed that even death could not separate them?

All these attempts at comfort, those beautiful words I just used, those abstract images, they are, of course, nothing more than ways to try to alleviate, perhaps to deal with the immense pain, with the horrors that the ears can no longer hear, to find comfort where it simply does not exist, because it isn't really about "death could not separate them," but the evil Hamas terrorists who brutally and mercilessly nailed them to the mattress by inserting metal wires into their bodies.

And yet, here we are, striving to be optimistic even though we can't find anything to console ourselves with, seeking to find the good in the bad, the angel in the devil, the humanity in cruelty.

Who knows? Maybe it's for the best because it shows who we are.

This is actually what separates us: those rational people who will try to find any way to suppress the horrors they have just heard from those monsters who delight in the creation of evil, who delight in causing death, and who choose abuse as their way of life.

So yes, there is probably some comfort after all, and it is that we are on the right side.

"They tied her to a tree and raped her."

"I was upset there, but so that you know, I don't get upset from seeing a corpse. I'm one of those people who can handle large quantities of corpses and not say a word. There were no corpses here, only abuse, crazy abuse, without anything that resembled humanity," Natan pointed out to me. "Imagine that you entered the scene in Kfar Aza a month after you had already removed the bodies from there. Parents and two children lay on the mattress, and on the mattress next to it lay another daughter. You pick up the mattress, and the mattress is still dripping with blood. A month later. A month!"

Natan told me about what happened, "The whole room was turned upside down because they shot at them indiscriminately. They didn't have time to abuse them, so they just shot all five members of the family and murdered them."

The horrors were far from over, and Natan continued to describe the days after the attack.

"On Sunday, October 8th, I found a girl who was tied to a tree. Her head was tied with a flannel rope. So were her eyes. She was tied to the head and was actually hanging on the tree. Her hands were tied back. She was completely naked. She had a cluster of bullets in her back, full of dry blows all over her body, and the whole pelvic area was... like... there's no question what happened there."

"What was in the pelvis? Do you mean sperm?" I didn't have time to complete the question.

Natan stopped me and replied, "There were many, many bruises on the pelvis and also cuts in this particular area. From here, you can understand what happened. Moreover, I only saw her back and not the front side. But what I saw from behind was enough for me to understand what happened, and in general, it was enough for me for many years."

"How many terrorists were there? Was it a gang rape?" I asked Natan, and he said that near the tree where she was found, several terrorists were killed, and their bodies were also there.

"When you tell me she was tied from her head, you mean she was bound with her body downward, almost leaning with her head against the tree?" I tried to find out how the rape actually took place.

He did not hesitate, got up from the chair and showed me exactly how she was found. He demonstrated how the girl was leaning on the tree, with her rear end pulled backward and her body facing the tree horizontally. She was actually in a bent position.

"She was tied from the head, so it looked like she was half standing, even though she was already dead," Natan said. "I drive on the roads, see girls and think about that situation. This is the first association that comes to my mind. I see girls walking in their neighborhood, and I just think about the fact that that girl was also in her neighborhood. I mean, it happened in her supposedly safe space," he said while moving his hands in different directions as a man seeking salvation.

Natan added that he had visited the same place where he had found that girl again, but the tree was no longer there this time.

"There was still fighting in that area, so the tree was likely cut down during one of the battles."

A question arises in my mind as to how a brutal and merciless gang rape helps to "free Palestine from the hands of the Zionists."

Probably, if we were to ask this question, even the most extreme on the Palestinian side would have a hard time answering.

"A leg, a hand, a head, a stomach. They cut off their limbs while they were still alive and scattered them around the house. The upper half of the body was in one room, and the lower half of the body in another room."

"There are cases where there is no doubt. Confirmation of death was not required because they simply cut a person in half. And yet, after they cut him in half, they shot him in the head to confirm the kill," Natan told me.

When I asked if he himself had witnessed such cases, he answered, "There were cases where I found different people's legs in different places, hands in different places, body parts in different places."

With great difficulty but eagerness to commemorate what happened, he continued, "I brought someone's hand from Kfar Aza to the funeral in Kibbutz Shafaim. His body was already on the way to the funeral, and I managed to arrive in time so that the hand would also be buried, of course, after identifying that it belonged to that person."

Natan said that even at the party in Re'im, he witnessed various body parts which were burned.

He also shared what he witnessed in Kibbutz Be'eri.

"Be'eri's houses are numbered by the hundreds, like in a hotel, where each floor has its own count accordingly. So, I arrived at the area where the buildings started with the number 500, where there were many burned houses. On the morning of October 9th, this was the area where I arrived to clear many dead people. In that area specifically, people were not only burned, but their limbs were also cut out. I mean, I took half a burned body from one room and half a burned body from another room. There were cases when I didn't even recognize if it was a man or a woman because the body was burned to the core."

Natan continued, "There were some who were also burned whole. But there were quite a few who were also burned, and their bodies were not whole. You see that those people had some 'work done on them' before the house was burned down. There was a case where I found half a burned upper body in one room and half a burned lower body in another room of the same person. There was a case where I found different limbs scattered in all the rooms of the house, but not a body."

I stopped him, asked, and insisted, "What limbs, for example?"

Natan didn't stop momentarily, "Arms, legs, head. An abdomen alone, just an abdomen, without arms and legs. Head alone, arms alone, legs alone. Even parts of the legs themselves separate. Some people were burned in a certain area of their body and nowhere else. Every house became a slaughterhouse. The burning was after they had abused them. They simply left the houses and burned them. After they left a human part here and a human part there, some rooms were burned more and rooms that were burned less."

I had to verify the process that took place.

"So, actually, you're telling me that they first cut off their limbs, they placed each limb in a different room, and finally, they burned the house?" I asked, wondering how profound evil runs.

Natan replied, "I don't know if they 'placed' them. There was one with half of one leg, for that matter. I mean, he only had one leg, but half of it. Maybe they took his leg off and just dragged it into the living room or the bedroom."

"So, you're basically saying they abused them while they were alive since the cremation was afterward," I said desperately to Natan, who was himself a nervous wreck.

"Obviously, the fire was afterward. Do you think they came in after the fire and removed their limbs?! There was no compassion. People were burned, cut in half, and amputated. I'm telling you again. A burned human being, half of his body in one room, the other half in another. Can you even imagine that?"

Alon Penzel

"Some of the burned children disintegrated in our hands. People's fingers were cut off with axes."

"Children, in the situations you've described, did you see them?" I asked Natan.

"The biggest group of children I saw consisted of burned children. Nine burned children in the children's home."

I gave Natan a hard time and asked him how they were burned and if they were found in one place.

Natan explained that it was impossible to understand what they saw in front of their eyes.

"Some of the kids were a little burned, and some of the kids disintegrated in your hands."

There was no time to stop and digest those chilling testimonies he told, and he had already gone on to more horrors.

"I saw the people that were abused. I saw people who had their fingers cut off finger by finger brutally, and marks and cuts were made on their bodies with a knife and all kinds of other tools."

I had to stop him and find out, "What do you mean? The terrorists cut his fingers off after they went into his home?"

There was silence in the room that lasted about twenty seconds.

On the one hand, Natan sighed, took the time to think, reflect, remember, and return to those unimaginable sights. On the other hand, I myself took the opportunity to take a few deep breaths before potentially entering another horror movie.

"One of the residents of Be'eri contacted me hoping to find her father. We arrived at his house. It was an apartment with several levels, including a living floor on the ground, a basement below the ground, and an attic above. The house was completely burned down. The only thing we found in this whole house was a faucet hanging on a burned wall in the kitchen. Apart from that, there was nothing, simply nothing. We couldn't find the father either," Natan said.

But the case did not end there. "The daughter insisted on continuing to look for her father. She told us that he managed to report to her before all communication was cut off. She said that he fought terrorists and apparently managed to kill some of them," he said.

But the fight against the terrorists did not end without a price.

Several terrorists managed to catch her father and cut off several of his fingers with an ax. The daughter said that even though his fingers were cut off, he was so determined that despite the shock that the terrorists inflicted on him, he still managed to escape from them, wounded and bleeding - he went back inside the house. According to the daughter, the communication between her and her father was gone at this stage.

The daughter continued to insist that they find her father dead or alive. She was adamant that he was at home, as they had been cut off after he reported to her that he had managed to escape back inside. Natan did report to her that the entire house was burned to the ground and that nothing was left, certainly not a body or a human corpse, but she did not give up.

Natan continued the story. "We returned to the house for the second time. In retrospect, we realize that he built himself a very special, almost impenetrable, safe room he ran to. The terrorists tried to shoot from all directions, but they were unable to penetrate the resistant safe room. That's why they decided to burn down the house. But his safe room was so protected," he said, "that even the fire could not penetrate it."

In those moments, I prayed that this story would have a happy ending, contrary to the vast majority of the testimonies. Finally, the miracles that happened on that cursed Sabbath would be revealed.

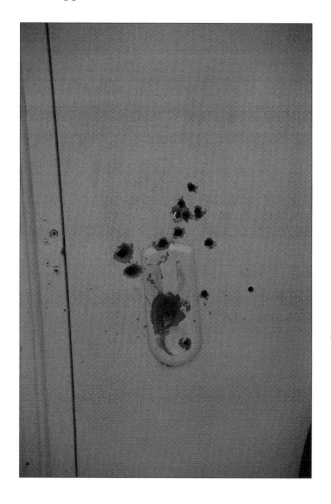

But apparently, happy endings only exist in movies or children's stories, and what happened on October 7th was anything but a miracle.

"They managed to insert smoke into the safe room. He died from that. When we found him, he was charred," Natan said. "The reason we didn't find him the first time is that everything in the house collapsed, and one of the walls that collapsed fell on the door of the safe room and hid it. Only a day later, and just because his daughter insisted so much, we went there and searched again. There was already a strange smell this time, so we started knocking and breaking the walls with different tools until one wall started moving. Then we discovered that there was a door hidden behind the wall - that's where we found him," he said.

"And what condition was he in when you found him?" I asked.

Natan said, "Like the daughter described. No fingers on his right hand. They cut them off. He was lying on the bed in a fetal position. He was charred."

So, yes. I was hoping for a "good ending - all is well," but I wasn't surprised deep down.

When it comes to the brutality of Hamas terrorists, miracles are not part of the package, certainly not mercy. As in the other horror stories here, too, we can only take solace in the fact that the body was found and was buried. It is true that this is such a small consolation, but one that, absurdly, quite a few of the victims of the Black Sabbath did not receive at all.

"He was tied up and naked. A metal object was inserted into his groin."

"I saw axes, hammers, hoes, and screwdrivers. I saw all kinds of tools stuck in people. Every tool you can imagine they used to stick inside people's bodies," Natan told me. "You witness with your own eyes continuous evil, evil after evil after evil. In Be'eri, there was a case where a mother and child were tied up and burned. You don't really know what happened. You only see the aftermath."

Natan also shared his feelings about the negotiations that took place with the terrorist organization Hamas through mediators such as Qatar and Egypt.

"The atrocities committed by the terrorists prove that they have no compassion. This is not a word they know. Even with enemies, we make peace because they are human beings. But these people are not human beings. That's why I cannot understand how anyone can keep negotiating and talking about a ceasefire with them. Yes, all the people should be brought home, but if I had the option... I... really..." He couldn't even finish the sentence out of rage.

He continued to describe the horrors he was exposed to in the kibbutzim.

"We entered one of the houses, to a scene where there were four bodies - an entire family. Three of the family members were found in one room. All of them were tied up and shot. Only the family's father was not in the same room with them. The father was actually in another room on the other side of the house, in the safe room. We found him completely naked and bound as well. The terrorists stuck all kinds of objects in his body. There was something stuck in his groin..."

Natan stopped talking. With great difficulty, he tried to show me with his hands what kind of object it was, but he could not say the word.

He lowered his hands back to his knees as if looking desperate, sighed lightly, and shook his head several times.

"You see... it's... they are animals... well, I'm telling you, they are animals. You know what? It's a certain type of animal that even the animals themselves don't recognize," he said in despair as he waved his hands in the air many times.

Despite the difficulty, and some would say even the audacity, I had to find out what really happened, what was inserted into that person's groin, but I couldn't find the words either, and muttered, "What did they put in his groin? Was it something sharp? Some kind of object?"

The room went silent for a few seconds. Natan rolled his eyes and replied, "Iron. A metal object."

"And how was he murdered? Was he also shot in the end?" I asked Natan.

He answered angrily, "Yes, in the end, he, too, was shot. Understand, there is no one who was not shot. Even the burned bodies had a bullet in their head." I reflect on Natan's words about the terrorists lacking any compassion and not being human at all. This testimony brutally proves his point. What compassion can be found in such a cruel situation? A father is separated from his family, tied up, stripped, and subjected to objects, including metal, being inserted into his body and private parts. Of course, they then murdered him and the rest of his family.

And here we are.

Another whole family that disappeared in the blink of an eye.

Another family that was slaughtered after being abused.

Another family that will not get to fulfill their dreams.

And perhaps more importantly - another painful, cruel, horrifying, and unimaginable memory from the October 7th holocaust.

The visual evidence

In recent months, I have been flooded with countless testimonies from various ZAKA volunteers who took time from their lives to share the horrors they witnessed so that October 7th, 2023, will forever be remembered as a national disaster for the State of Israel and the Jewish people.

Between testimonies, between stories, between burned babies and mothers who will not return to take care of their small children, I was also exposed to exclusive visual testimonies that were filmed in the field in real moments under inferno and terror by various ZAKA volunteers and members of the security and rescue forces.

Those hard-to-view videos and photos have been extensively verified and will now be brought into writing.

"What does it look like, guys?" One of the women present shouted into the air.

Natan replied unambiguously, "It's a corpse. What could it be? It looks relatively small for a man, but we'll soon know."

In front of me was the video taken in Kibbutz Be'eri in the days after the brutal surprise attack. I watched the exclusive video over and over to understand precisely what was in front of me and what I was witnessing.

Not only were the sights unimaginable, but they were also challenging to understand and identify. Next to a large number of ZAKA volunteers who are trying to extract body parts from the ruins, you can only see a small skull, smaller than you can imagine, completely burned, buried in the ground. You can see the small eyes, nose, and mouth structure. It seems like a baby or a small child, but it is not yet known.

"We are digging and digging, and there is another body in Kibbutz Be'eri. We are working extremely carefully to bring everyone to a burial, every human part, everyone possible," Natan said as he stood in front of the ruins.

One of the other volunteers, who "worked" on the same body, informed his friends that he "found a bone."

In another video, which was also filmed in Be'eri, ZAKA volunteers are seen trying to rescue small bodies of children from the decomposed and burnt ruins.

The bodies in the video, if you can understand what is happening in it at all, looked so small and so different in shape from an average human body that it was difficult for me to really understand what was in front of me. Even through the camera lens, the lighter parts of their bodies revealed the evil and cruelty with which those children were murdered.

We have already been exposed to the dental clinic in Kibbutz Bari that the ZAKA volunteers mentioned many times in their testimonies, the same clinic where no less than seven children were slaughtered, or rather what was left of them. But for the first time, I was also exposed to exclusive documentation from the moments of entering that clinic, which became the scene of an inhuman massacre.

At the entrance to the clinic, there were slingshots, grenades, knives, bags, vests, radios, weapon cartridges and a lot of ammunition.

Already from outside the clinic, you could see the heavy destruction left by the terrorists, but when you got inside, you realized that nothing was left. No product, object or tool remained intact. It can be described as utter destruction. You couldn't find an empty space on the floor to walk on, as the ruins were everywhere. The floor was still covered in blood. The walls are destroyed, charred, and broken, as are the chairs, the boxes, or any other equipment you can imagine.

"There is a cartridge, a weapon and a grenade without its security pin inside the refrigerator," the ZAKA volunteers and the IDF soldiers who were inside the building in real-time shouted.

The scenes from the dental clinic completely corresponded with Reuven's testimony that the terrorists did everything in their power to harm the rescue teams that they knew would arrive afterward.

"There is the smell of a corpse in here," one of the ZAKA volunteers in one of the other videos described while walking next to a safe room that had blown out of its place. Needless to say, it was completely broken. The volunteer was sure of himself: "There is the smell of a corpse in this safe room. I tell you, there is something here. This safe room has a smell, guys."

On leaving Kfar Aza, you could see a long, very long line of soldiers covered in bags whose faces we will never see again.

Along with the same sights and smells in the kibbutzim, there was also the party in Re'im.

Unimaginable sights, such as I was exposed to at the International Holocaust Museum in Washington DC, United States. You could see "slaughter carts" being driven to the trucks. Body on top of body on top of body. Men on women, and women on men with and without clothes, bleeding in most parts of their bodies.

In those seconds, I couldn't help but think about the death pits of the Holocaust or the gas trucks because there was no difference between the testimonies, between the pictures, and the sights. Bodies lie side by side after they are collected. Who can imagine that those guys were on their feet and dancing just a few moments ago? Deep inside, I wanted to imagine those young people lying there because they went to sleep after a long and fun party. But the fields, the grass, and the soil that was reddened with blood left no room for doubt. There was a massacre here. A brutal massacre the likes of which has never been seen in Israel.

As we know, Hamas's atrocities were not limited to the Ra'im festival and kibbutzim. They also took place on the roads. The same infernal roads we mentioned, mainly Road 232 and Road 34, which surround the Gaza border.

In photos that couldn't even be compared to civil wars in different parts of the world, I witnessed bodies lying all along the road in a video that was taken on Sunday, October 8th.

Twenty-four hours from the start of the event and in the sovereign state of Israel, the bodies of men and women are lying in the middle and on the sides of a major road without anyone tending to them.

On the roads, there were vast amounts of bodies scattered everywhere, but at this stage, there was no one to take care of them, nor was there enough equipment.

"You can't leave them lying in the street like that," a ZAKA volunteer shouted into the air after his request to receive equipment supplies for the bleeding roads was denied more than twenty-four hours after the event began.

"There is nothing to do," answered other volunteers, who themselves were cruel victims of the situation they found themselves in.

As you read these words, take a deep breath.

Try to imagine and feel the same images deep in your heart - the burnt bodies of the children and those lying on the road. Try to imagine a hoe or an ax covered with body parts and internal organs of a child, a woman, or maybe an elderly person. Try to imagine the dismembered bodies of those who were burned, those who were shot and those who were strangled to death.

Try to unite with the pain of those people, with the horrors, with the fear.

Try to understand that it's not just about pictures but a sad reality that happened not far from you.

Try to understand the magnitude of the war crimes committed by Hamas's terrorists and the importance of commemorating those war crimes.

Now stop.

Take a deep breath once again, and now try to imagine and feel, but this time, try to imagine those children who ran in the fields and played with their little brothers, the mothers and fathers who changed the diapers of their tiny babies, the "goodbye" kiss of that mother on her son's forehead just before he entered the kindergarten, the loving hug of that little boy to his father when he came home.

It is our eternal duty to remember and commemorate them in both ways. The way they lived and also the way they were murdered - there is no contradiction here.

It is our duty to make sure that while we remember good and simple memories from 'before,' that is, before October 7th, we also commemorate what happened to them at the time of their murder. The abuse, the rape, the slaughter, the looting, the systematic murder, the strangulation, the burning, the shooting, the dismemberment, and all other things that happened to the victims of Hamas.

It is our duty to do so now and forever.

Chapter Two

Evidence from the "Forensic Medicine Institute"

Niccolò Machiavelli was an Italian statesman who believed that social relations are built on conflicting interests.

According to him, all social relationships are built based on fear, power, strength, and deterrence. Machiavelli discussed the various circumstances in which a citizen can become a leader and rise to power, and raised questions regarding the just, proper, and correct way to lead people and how to rule them according to changing circumstances.

Machiavelli's doctrine is not ambiguous. In his writings, he believed that a leader should impose his will on the people and that the real job of the leader is to be a soldier, to engage in systematic and continuous violence, which includes destruction, war, curfew, imprisonment, torture, abuse and more, and with the understanding that a leader's only resource is physical strength.

The leader must be cruel and brutal and not allow unnecessary considerations of justice, morality, or values. According to him, only in this way will the leader achieve a long tenure and make far-reaching changes in his country.

Machiavelli's philosophy can very easily be paralleled to Hamas's relationship with the residents of the Gaza Strip and in general.

Hamas imposed its will on the residents in a dictatorial manner, at the very least, and did not leave them with any choices. Hamas did indeed engage in systematic violence, the kind that is also characteristic within the Strip, to anyone who has made up his mind to rebel. We will not argue about the fact that Hamas's activists, led by the leaders of the terrorist organization, see force, power, cruelty, and brutality as the only way to a just solution, and certainly, there is no place in the organization for values of justice or morality.

But Machiavelli did not stop there.

He believed that in certain countries or territories, the people would be loyal to the leader under normal and stable conditions. He called these static conditions "when death is far away, and the citizens need the state," when there is no danger to the citizens and when the citizens need a central government. In such situations, the people will remain loyal to the leader.

But what will happen in times of trouble?

After all, the citizens of the country remain loyal to the leader for one reason only: they fear him, and they are driven by the desire to stay alive.

But what will happen when the lives of those citizens are threatened by a third party—a threat greater than the threat posed by the leader? Will the country's citizens then remain loyal, or will they rebel under the circumstances?

Machiavelli believed that in such a brutal form of government, the citizens are, in fact, mercenaries of the state and not genuinely loyal to it. Few will choose to stay by its side. Therefore, he claimed that a wise leader would be the one to think of a system where, in both regular times and crises, the citizens would always need him, and the state would thus always be loyal to him.

The questions remain:

It is a new threat (that third party) that the residents of the Gaza Strip face (lack of food, water, fuel, housing, electricity, gas and even them being used as a human shield), and all of their suffering which the terrorist organization Hamas is responsible for, especially now, overcome the threat that Hamas's operatives posed to them in general during regular times?

Will the mercenaries, who are residents of the Gaza Strip, remain loyal to the Hamas organization, or will they rebel against it?

Will the mortal blow that Hamas inflicted on the residents of the Gaza Strip in the October 7th attack be the last nail in the coffin of the murderous terrorist organization that considers the murder of other people's children a higher value than preserving the lives of its own children?

The evidence from the "Forensic Medicine Institute."

"The Forensic Medicine Institute" is the only public institution in Israel that provides forensic medicine services.

The institute, also known as the "National Center for Forensic Medicine," is located in Tel Aviv's Abu Kabir neighborhood. Its primary function is to investigate the causes and mechanisms of death through postmortem inspection.

According to the Ministry of Health, the institute also "assists in the investigation of serious crime cases such as murder, through DNA tests, and finding a connection between the findings at the scene and the body involved in the incident, identifying victims and unknowns, assisting in locating missing persons, examining bodies and providing a professional opinion."

Since October 7th, the Institute of Forensic Medicine in Israel has been an integral part of the Sisyphean effort to identify the bodies of the murdered and victims in numbers that the State of Israel has never faced. Unlike most cases in the past, this time, the institute's work involves mental difficulties that its employees were not ready for due to unimaginable sights and horrors that are difficult to view and describe and will be detailed in the upcoming testimonies.

To gain more insight, I met with Doctor Chen Kugel, the head and director of the Institute of Forensic Medicine.

"I started October 7th at home; it was just another Saturday. Little by little, we began to understand that a multi-casualty event was developing, but at the time, we didn't understand to what extent," Chen said. At approximately 2:00 p.m., midday of Saturday, we gathered all the institute employees and prepared to receive the bodies here at the Forensic Medicine Institute in Tel Aviv, according to the procedure."

As per usual, in every other incident that happened in Israel in the past, even in incidents with many casualties, Chen and his employees handled the bodies in the institute itself, but this time, the institute's employees, led by Chen, did not yet understand the magnitude of the Black Sabbath disaster. "At first, they talked about a hundred people, then about a hundred and fifty. When we realized that these were such large numbers, we started organizing special refrigerated containers because we didn't have storage space for such a large number of bodies. We organized the division and the work method among ourselves, but over time, we realized that it was not a hundred or one hundred and fifty bodies but much more. The magnitude of the disaster, which already sounded cruel to us at the time, only continued to become clearer as time passed. At this stage, we already understood that there was no place to store the number of bodies that came and that work could not be done here, so a decision was made to move it to Camp Shura, in the south of the country," he said.

According to Chen, the decision to transfer the work to Shura was indeed correct, but it was not an institute of forensic medicine. Shura is a place intended for refrigerating corpses, and it has a large storage space, yet the number of corpses was so huge that there was not enough space to store all of them there either. On top of that, Camp Shura did not have the necessary professional work tools found at the institute in Tel Aviv.

"In the first few days, the bodies were indeed moved to Shura, and there they began to inspect each body at a time from start to finish literally 'by the book.' Each body that came in went through an orderly process that included registration of the clothes, the objects that were in its possession, photographed documentation of the body, fingerprints, dental radiography, taking DNA samples, examination of external signs, X-ray of the whole body and more. After that, the body went out to the refrigerators," Chen elaborated and said that at that stage, the institute's role was mainly to supervise what was being done to see if any assistance, counseling, etc., was needed.

Chen also said that in the early days, the institute's work was not particularly busy, which is why he insisted that the work was not being done correctly, given the circumstances.

"At those moments, I told them the work method was incorrect. The orderly process of treating a body takes about one hour, and at that rate, we would have finished the work after maybe two months. It wouldn't have allowed us to work on all the cases."

After four days of persuasion, Chen's suggestion was finally accepted.

They comprehensively took the fingerprints of all the bodies in the containers and a DNA sample from each of them. In this way, according to Chen, the laboratories of the Institute of Forensic Medicine could start working simultaneously with the laboratories in Shura.

"The laboratories here at the institute started working on the DNA samples that came from those bodies, and the work in Shura also continued at the same time. Thus, anyone who could not be identified in that orderly process in Shura because they were burned or something similar was transferred to the Institute of Forensic Medicine," Chen said.

Indeed, a week later, the majority of work moved to the Institute of Forensic Medicine in Tel Aviv.

The workers opened all the body bags that were in the containers and took DNA samples and fingerprints from all of them.

"There was a very massive workload for two days. All the body bags were opened," Chen continued, "as soon as we started to understand that there were bodies that could not be identified based on the samples, and it is understandable why, then the case was passed to us."

I immediately asked Chen which bodies had arrived at the institute and why. I mean, what was the condition of those bodies so that they could not identify them?

Chen quickly replied, "All the bodies that were burned. Completely burned, or burned to the extent that they couldn't extract DNA samples from them. There were also completely rotten bodies, or bodies that came in parts."

"So, these were the three main cases: burnt, rotten bodies and those that arrived in parts?"

I insisted on getting a precise explanation from Chen, who replied, "There were all kinds. We started working around the clock. I saw both corpses and corpse parts. In one case, we received a black lump of coal. Only after we took an X-ray could we understand that the same lump of coal was actually two different people. An older woman and a younger woman who were hugging. Their condition was such that they hugged while they were being burned, and around them was a metal wire that tied them together. We know that they were burned alive because they have soot in their tracheas."

The story touched me immediately.

I couldn't help but stop Chen and ask him to see the bodies myself. A moment later, I wondered if I'd made a mistake by damaging my soul that way and how much I would regret it later.

But there was not much time to think.

I stared at that black lump. The horror was evident at first glance. It was a completely blackened block of coal, separated in two at the top but connected as one body.

Though nothing can be said for sure, but when I looked carefully, it seemed that they had tiny heads and hands that indeed tried to hug each other. With the exception of those unclear expressions on that burnt block, I am confident that if they had put it on a barbecue, I would have thought it was coal, and nothing could have been seen.

Chen also allowed me to see the X-rays taken of that burnt block, photographs based on which the institute's researchers determined that these were indeed two women.

"After seeing the bodies, look at the X-rays, and you will see that two spines can be identified. One young and one old person with two sets of ribs, and around them, you see the metal wire that I told you with which they were tied," he told me as I looked with stunned eyes at the unusual X-rays.

He said that there were also other bodies that did not have soot in their trachea. In this case, Chen's staff members could determine that those people were burned after death. That is, they were murdered in some other way, and then they (the terrorists) went to the trouble of burning their bodies.

"Some of the fires were very, very massive because there are quite a few cases where we couldn't extract DNA from the bodies, and that doesn't just happen usually. A person doesn't get burned like that normally. We've seen people burned in the past in car accidents or house fires. They do get burned, but we can still extract

DNA from them. But when it's over seven hundred degrees for a long time, DNA cannot be extracted," Chen said.

The question is how those bodies came to be cremated at seven hundred degrees. Chen answered with a pained expression, "The most prominent possibility that we know happened is that the terrorists deliberately added a lot of burning materials so that something like a crematorium would be created. The bones we got were bones that crumbled, bones that had nothing left of them, bones that we could not sample and wouldn't help us identify the victim. Our job in these cases is to look for thicker bones where the inside didn't get that hot, and even then, it's terribly difficult, and in some cases, we don't succeed at all."

Among the harrowing testimonies, I continued to see the horrors with my own eyes. That's when Chen showed me another case.

"This is a closed bag that came from a safe room. When we opened the bag, this is what we saw."

I looked and was horrified.

I stopped breathing for a few seconds.

Again, I couldn't believe my own eyes. This time, two small, black lumps lay in front of me - completely separated, unlike the previous lump. In this case, I couldn't really identify anything. At first glance, I could only assume that it was a head and another body part or two heads of two different people.

Besides the black lumps, there were also some kinds of white parts whose content I could not understand until Chen explained them to me.

"Those are two black lumps and white bones. If we separate them, as we did the white bones, which look like white coals in a way, they're a human being, or rather what's left of it. The bones right next to them belong to the other person. Two people were there."

Chen explained that in this case, the institute's employees were unable to find DNA because the body was completely burned. "Like coals," Chen told me.

I replied, "Like coals on a barbecue, that's what's left of these people."

I continued my conversation with Chen and insisted on understanding.

"You have a burned body. A lump of coal, as you describe it. You now have to look for tissues inside this lump. How do you do that?"

Chen replied, "We're looking for tissues that haven't been completely burned. If it's a black lump, it's likely that we'll find something inside it. The problem is mainly with all kinds of bones, which are burnt bones with nothing left of them. It looks like something white. White coals, as I said."

He continued to describe the atrocities and emphasized the brutality of the Hamas terrorists, "It is very difficult to create bodies that look like the ones we found. Either you use very special weapons, or you use incendiary materials. We know that they added more and more combustibles, such as fuel and tires, to burn the bodies even more."

Chen claimed that the brutality and lack of mercy can be seen right in the bodies themselves, "Some people were shot while they were handcuffed and tied. That is, people who got handcuffed with anything they found, whether it was zip-ties they brought or whether it was an electrical cord of a kettle they found at the house. They tied those people's hands, and while that bound group of people was sitting there together, the terrorists went to each of them and shot them in the head or the back of the head. These are people who were simply executed by shooting at point-blank range."

The horror didn't end there.

Chen said that there were bodies on which you can see that the people were murdered by many different methods, "A single person was burned, stabbed, shot, and run over with a car. You see people who had their heads taken off. Many people arrive without their heads. Some people not only got their legs taken off, but they literally crushed them so they couldn't walk, and then locked them in some place so they would die from loss of blood."

Chen believed that everything was planned. "When someone is shot in the middle of a war, the mental energy is not invested in brutalizing them. In the case of the Black Sabbath, the terrorists spent time making the victims suffer. We see severed limbs and can't even tell what the terrorists did to cut off those limbs or if it was done while the victims were alive, because the corpses were brought to us in a rotting state - but the point is that we see severed limbs such as legs for example."

For me to understand what he meant by rotten corpses, Chen showed them to me.

I tried to understand what I was seeing.

"What is this?" I asked with the innocence of a small child.

"This is a rotten corpse," replied Chen.

I looked and saw a body. This one was mostly intact, but its color did not resemble a human color. It seemed like the skin was peeled and had a hideously silver tone. The back of the head was broken from the inside and out, and holes could be seen on the nape of the neck. The hands were blackened, and maybe it just seemed that the arms were smaller than they should be.

Chen informed me about the case.

"At the back of the neck, you can see the gunshot wounds. And if you look closely, you will see that the body's hands are tied up with zip-ties, and these zip-ties were connected to other zip-ties behind the back."

I tried to find out with the head of the institute how severed bodies are handled.

"If, for example, you come to a row of legs detached from a body or a head detached, how do you recognize what belongs to who?"

Chen said that many such bodies came to him.

"To date, the institute has examined about 1,200 body bags, so you ask yourself how it can be as there are not 1,200 bodies. The answer is that each body bag does not necessarily contain only one person. There are body bags that contain organs and limbs from several people, and there are many, many people who come scattered in several body bags. We still receive bones here and bones there. Some of them are people we have already identified and are in the grave, and they were simply scattered in all kinds of places, so we find parts of their bodies after they have already been buried."

I asked Chen how they identify a person when only a skull comes to them, and he replied, "You take a DNA sample. If it's a skull with teeth, you can, perhaps, identify it by teeth. But if it doesn't have teeth, then you identify it by DNA. Some people have very, very few parts of the skull left. For example, some people are buried with only fifteen to twenty grams of their total body. That's all that was left of them. But how do I know they're dead? Because it's bones from the skull, and I know you can't live without these bones, even though these bones are so small, the size of a fingernail, you can tell that without them, these people are not alive, even though nothing else is found of their body. So, you can determine their death in this way."

Chen found it essential to emphasize once again that everything was planned. According to him, the terrorists were systematic in their actions.

"There are bodies that were shot at; there are bodies that were tied up and shot at. Some bodies got burned. I mean, each group had its own method of murder. It was something planned. This is not an individual incident where a terrorist went into a 'tantrum' and decided to commit atrocities at that moment. Absolutely not. The terrorists knew in advance that they were coming to participate in a horrific journey. They came with the fuel tanks to burn. You can see in every group of murdered people that there was some terrorist that told his "crew" exactly how to carry out the murders."

I couldn't help but ask Chen about children and babies.

"Yes, we saw children. Some of the children were burned, and I didn't know why they didn't have a head. Is it because of the fire, or maybe because of a missile that hit them? I know that some children had their heads decapitated. I saw a girl about twelve years old who certainly was decapitated by the terrorists. They shot her in the head and then took it off her."

After he told me about that twelve-year-old girl whose head was cut off came the moment I was not prepared for.

It is a moment that will be etched in my heart forever.

Sights that will never leave my mind.

These sights were witnessed by many people who worked tirelessly on the unimaginable tasks that had to be done in the inferno of the Black Sabbath.

Sights from which there is no way back.

There was no way to misunderstand what lay in front of me: a twelve-year-old girl who was rotten, partly decapitated, crushed, deformed. She stared at me while I looked at her.

Her body was muddy from decay. The head was torn from its place, completely cut off. One tiny piece of tissue on the side of the neck still connected what was left of the body to what was left of the head. The face and nose are entirely wrinkled. Her eyes seemed to pop out of place, or so it seemed. The face was distorted in an alien way that aroused disgust and repulsion. The mouth and cheeks were completely crushed.

A character from a horror movie. Worse. I think that it would have been censored in the cinema. However, the huge difference is that this was not a movie - but a very cruel reality.

As mentioned, the body was almost completely detached from the head - so they could clearly see that her throat had been cut at the neck. A little hair, also gray, remained on her head.

"This is the girl I told you about," Chen said.

I stuttered and asked, "I see the head is almost completely torn off, but some connection remains."

He nodded, "They cut her throat. A piece of skin remained, a piece of tissue."

I stopped Chen again, forcefully preventing him from speaking as if I didn't want to hear anymore. Yet, I had to. So, after a moment, I continued to ask questions like a scared little child who doesn't understand what he sees in front of him.

"Why does her face look like that?" I asked in a whisper, perhaps apprehensively.

"It's rotting," Chen replied, "but rotting is one thing. What's unusual here is that, as you can see, they cut off her head."

Though I struggled, we continued the testimony.

I asked him to tell me about the rape cases.

"There were cases of rape on October 7th, rape that came before the kill. And you, as pathologists, have to decide if rape was done and how it was done. How do you determine what happened when a body arrives burned, rotten, or cut?"

Chen didn't like the question but didn't hesitate, "I have something to say about it. It makes me very angry when people ask me for evidence of rape. I mean very angry. After all, we know very well that only a small percentage of rape cases have forensic evidence. In most cases, such conclusive evidence does not exist because the genitals are built for sex, so it is unlikely that there will always be an injury there. Even if there is sperm, extracting it as time passes is complicated. And here, the international community is asking us for proof. The videos are not enough, the testimonies of the survivors are not enough, and suddenly they are asking us for evidence that there was rape because otherwise, as far as they are concerned, it did not happen. Because Hamas, as we know, can kidnap babies and shoot the elderly but rape?! How can such a thing be believed?" Chen said sarcastically while raising his hands in the air in great anger.

Indeed, there were videos and not only that.

I also witnessed the testimonies that came from the field about rape, testimonies heard from the mouths of ZAKA volunteers in this very book.

"In the labs, of course, we couldn't check for evidence of rape at all because the bodies were rotten and burned," Chen concluded.

He presented me with another bag from Shura that came to them.

"As you can see, there are black coals here, not burned," and I saw them. "We took a CT scan. You can see long bones of limbs and skull bones in front of you," Chen said while looking at those 'black coals.' In fact, those black lumps were not burned. The CT scans actually explain what was found in them.

"Tell me about cases of impossible identification, those cases that, even after you've tried everything, still couldn't be identified," I asked.

"On the one hand, there is a list of missing persons, and on the other hand, there is a list of bodies," replied Chen and continued, "There are bodies that we have not been able to identify even though we have been able to extract DNA, and we still do not know who the person is. The first possibility is that it is a terrorist. The second possibility is someone who has not been reported as a missing person at all. For example, during the return of the abductees, three Thai citizens returned; the authorities here did not know at all that they had been kidnapped because no one reported their absence. These are illegal workers, so the employers did not report it at all, and then people you didn't even know were kidnapped and returned. By the same logic, the same could also happen with a dead body."

I stopped him and insisted on finding out.

"But what about the opposite case? If you have the name of a person who is missing, but all along you are unable to identify him, find his body, or a part of it, some body part that you can associate with him, what do you do then?"

Chen folded his arms on his chest and replied, "We are constantly receiving bones from which DNA cannot be extracted because they are too burnt, because it does not exist in them. With its resources, the IDF decided to send these cases to the most advanced and well-regarded laboratories abroad, but they, too, failed to extract DNA. It just doesn't exist."

I was also interested in hearing from Chen regarding the identification of the abductees, including Shani Louk, whose death was determined even though her body had not yet been found.

"Regarding the abductees, we don't know who is alive and who is dead. We know that there are dead abductees, and we have also determined their death even though they are not here. In the case of Shani Louk, we found a tiny part of her skull bone in one of the fields, even though her body is in Gaza. We checked the same part and saw in the DNA that it belonged to the Shani. Based on that, I determined that she was dead; this is because the part that was found was part of the base of the skull. You cannot live without this part unless they removed it in a very complex operation, one that was certainly not done on her in the field, and of course, she did not receive medical treatment after that. Therefore, it can be determined that she died."

Chen showed me with his hand how small the found piece was and said, "This is what was buried. A piece like this."

Following what he told me about how death can be determined based on small parts of the same human body, I had to find out if and how this can be done even when nothing is found.

"Are there cases where you don't determine death because you couldn't find the particles or organs that you said could help to determine if that person is not alive?"

"There are cases in which we found nothing, neither a body nor body parts and yet we can determine death. This is based on videos published by Hamas, Israeli security cameras, or any other information that comes in and can unequivocally determine that the person is dead. There are also cases where there is no way of knowing if the person is dead or not, but I'm sure that some of the abductees, and maybe a large part of them, are indeed dead. There are also people who we think were not kidnapped. We still can't find their parts and continue to look for them," Chen said while I was wondering if Hamas videos can indeed be a reliable enough source to determine the death of an Israeli citizen, a question that will probably echo in your mind as well.

Chen concluded, "It could very well be that we won't identify everyone either. Honestly, I'm sure not everyone will be identified in the end. I'm sure of it."

While feeling that I had already heard and seen the worst of all, Chen continued to share with me more horrors that took place on the Black Sabbath, horrors that the dedicated workers of the institute treated.

"If you look here, you can see three left legs and two right legs."

As I stared at them, I could clearly identify that these were legs, of course, completely severed without any other body part, but they looked different from what legs were supposed to look like. They were shrunken, black, tiny, burnt, and distorted in appearance. The small size of the feet forced me to turn to Chen and ask, "But how are they so small? I guess these are pieces of legs, not a whole leg."

Chen replied, "Of course. These are pieces of legs. These are legs that were burned, and in fact, we are talking about three different people who are in one body bag."

I took a deep breath and tried to think about the fact that instead of the small bag in front of me, where pieces of amputated, completely burned legs were held, three people used to be alive. Real human beings they probably had families that loved them. They are human beings whose remains are little pieces of coal. Nothing more.

I turned to Chen and asked him about his personal feelings.

"You told me you haven't seen such things in thirty-one years in this line of work. What do you mean? The forms these bodies were found in? The way those people were abused? Describe to me what touches you most about this whole story?"

Chen didn't think twice, "I've seen people burned and shot in the past, even people who exploded. But the brutality and system-aticity of the murder. The killings, cutting off the heads, tying people up and then shooting them, people who were shot through their hands because they tried to defend themselves while being shot at. Not only that, but the knowledge that everything was planned, precise and cold, not out of some specific storm of emotions. In the past, I have seen isolated cases like this, usually carried out by crazy people, mentally ill on a severe level. But on the Black Sabbath, you can see that it was something planned. These people did not have a mental illness. They did it to humili-ate, strike fear and abuse."

The helplessness described by Chen, where people raised their hands to shield their faces just before they were shot, shocked me.

I wanted to understand what it looked like.

Once again, the sights were hard to see.

"They (the terrorists) shot their hands because they were defending themselves at the time," he said. I looked at the shot and already rotten hands.

Even the fingers looked strange. When I looked at the gunshot wounds on the hands, I realized again the brutality of those terrorists. But mostly, I tried to feel and unite with the helplessness of those people who had nothing left to do but cover their faces with their hands and pray for salvation that did not come.

"Remember I told you about people who suffered from multiple methods of death?" Chen asked me while pointing at another dead body, "This is one of them."

I saw a completely burnt, scorched human body. His legs had been amputated, and one of his arms was positioned in a way that didn't seem natural for a human body; it was also broken. The hand on that arm was hard to recognize, if it was there at all. His face was distorted, and most horrifying of all, there was a large, unexplainable hole in the center of his body through which his internal organs should have been visible. The thing is that there was nothing inside. Not one organ. The only thing that seemed to be left were bones.

"You can also see the stab wounds on his body," Chen told me while pointing to the obvious stab marks.

"But what is it? There is a hole in the middle of his body!" I turned to Chen, anxious to understand why.

"It's because of the burn. The burn causes the tissues to rupture." Chen also showed me the CT scans of that person. "You can see his pelvis, which is completely broken. It is important to understand that this is not a fracture of the pelvis resulting from a fall - but that he was run over. You can also see the bullets inside his spine. So yes, he was shot, stabbed, burned, and also ran over," he said as he counted with his fingers the number of murder methods committed on that person. Chen continued to tell me about what he had witnessed.

"There are quite a few people that were fused together while they got burned, so they were also buried together. In some of these situations, people had to be taken out of the grave because we found only after the burial that the fused lump contained several people and not just one person."

I asked him to tell me about a specific example.

"In Shura, they didn't do CT scans, and we did. We had the ability to understand that it wasn't one person but several from the scans. In one case, several people were murdered in a car. They were burned. All the people in the car were identified except for one girl. At the institute, we understood that the girl was apparently buried with another person. We researched that case deeply and assumed that she was buried with a body that was identified as someone else's. We opened their grave, did CT scans of what came out of the grave and found two bodies there. Of course, not whole bodies, but body parts."

Following the conversation between Chen and me about the October 7th rape testimonies, and following the testimonies I've gathered (and will be revealed later in this very book) about the removal of male genital organs during the massacre, I asked Chen what was done in a situation where only a genital organ is found? How can it be associated with a body?

He explained that if there is DNA, it is possible to know the organ's identity. "The DNA in the penis is the same as in any other organ."

But since those genitals had been amputated, I felt the need to inquire with him about their burial.

"Can the genitalia of those men be buried with the rest of their bodies, perhaps their full bodies?"

Chen replied, "A genital organ will not survive long outside because it is a soft tissue that rots and eventually disintegrates. But yes, in principle, we try to attach the body parts to other parts that have already been buried, whether it is a genital organ or bones."

I presented to Chen an ethical-moral question about what should be done when body parts are found and associated with a person who has already been identified and has already been buried and even has a tombstone.

"In such a situation, we ask the family if we should reopen the grave and bury that organ in the same grave or if we should leave the grave as it is and bury the organ in a general grave. We receive both answers from the families."

Just before we continued our conversation, he showed me yet again some unimaginable sights that became a painful reality for many.

"As you can see, here is a body tied with some electric wire that the terrorists found in the house," Chen told me while I looked at the body that was indeed tied with the electric wire both in her hands and around the body itself. The body seemed completely rotten all over. Chen continued describing that body, "Here there is a gunshot wound to the head," pointing to the area, and I could only stare at the mouth that remained utterly open and the eyes in which the pupils could not be recognized, at least that's how it seemed at first glance.

"Here, as you can see, another body is tied with an electric wire."

I looked at the body, and after a short time, I turned to him with a question.

"The marks, the stains that are on the body, are from the fire, I assume?"

Chen shook his head. "No. These are rotten corpses. The skin peels off due to decay. It's not a burnt corpse."

Indeed, it turned out that the stains on the body, stains in a variety of horrific colors, were caused by decay. While looking at the corpse's crushed head, Chen explained to me, "Here he has a shot in the head. Can you see it?"

I, unfortunately, answered yes.

"Here, you can see another body tied up with zip-ties, and they just shot her in the head." Chen showed me the body that looked exactly like he described but with scary decay.

He also had some criticism of the police work done in Shura. First, because the bodies were examined only for the purpose of identification, the investigative need to collect evidence from the bodies and document the findings was completely neglected, which will make legal proceedings more difficult in the future.

Also, in the identification aspect, according to Chen, the results could have been better because, for example, many bodies were not stripped or even turned over. According to him, some bodies have not been identified, and it could have been if they just took off their clothes.

"We could have worked much better and much faster," he said, but he also emphasized, "In the end, the end results are respectable. Nowhere in the world have they identified such many bodies so quickly."

Finally, I tried to understand Chen's private state of mind and the state of mind of the other institute employees.

"Is it different from other times? How have you been with all of this?" I asked.

Chen said that the situation is completely different from previous events because the stories behind the sights are difficult stories. He also noted the workload, the quantity of bodies, and the fact that the work never ends.

"I am an old man, but a young person like you never felt a real existential threat; you never felt that there was really a threat to your life. And I think that in this case, we all suddenly felt that the situation was different this time. This time, it is not a joke. This time, it could have been me. This burnt person could have been me. We all feel and know that if the terrorists had advanced a little more, or if the attack had come from the Judea and Samaria region, the people there could have died too." He concluded, "There is also a feeling that the State of Israel is suddenly not such a safe place. Suddenly, we realize that we are fighting for our lives. Add to that that you keep hearing about what these monsters have done, and we see it with our own eyes. It's hard, challenging. Although in the autopsy room, you don't think about it, but later, when you hear the stories behind the bodies, you see it again in your imagination, and it feels terrible."

Sometimes, it seems that the disaster that has befallen the people of Israel is so great that there is no way back from it. It is a feeling that not only the people who lost their loved ones in the war may share but also the citizens of the entire country. The employees of the Forensic Medicine Institute are undoubtedly an integral part of those who witnessed the historical evil of Hamas terrorists and are at the top of the list of people who may lose hope in humanity.

And how can they be blamed? After all, it seems that the things they saw and dealt with constitute an eternal injury to the soul of an average person. One can only imagine how those workers return home at the end of the day and meet their families with everything they witnessed still lingering in their minds.

It is important to understand that the work of the institute's employees, and of all the security and rescue forces in general that worked during the events of October 7th and after them, is unbearably difficult not only because of the unimaginable sights, which would be difficult to find even in horror movies but also, and perhaps mainly because of the stories that stand behind those sights. The whole families of which nothing is left, the innocent smile on the faces of small children, a smile that will never return, the mothers who lost their sons, the fathers who lost their daughters, grandmothers and grandfathers who disappeared from their grandchildren's lives.

In all those unbearably difficult stories stand not only the victims who were murdered, and not even just their families but everyone who was touched in one way or another by the evilest and cruel terrorist attack the modern world has known.

As citizens of this blood-stained country, we can only cross our fingers and hope that our strength is indeed in our unity, that we will indeed find the way to rise from the dirt and see the light at the end of the tunnel.

We do not know how long it will take and if it will happen at all.

As mentioned, we do not live in a utopian world where there is a promise that good wins in the end, that the light prevails over the darkness, and that the power of the angel is stronger than the power of the devil.

And despite that, even though the promise of a better future does not exist, we are obligated to try and create that future. We must make sure that those people who were brutally murdered and those families who were separated from their loved ones did not sacrifice themselves in vain. Our commitment is to find a way to rise and shine for them.

Until then, and even when the moment comes, and it will happen, we will always be there to remember, commemorate, and talk about them.

Now and forever.

Chapter Three

Testimonies from Nova Survivors

J ohn Rawls was an American philosopher who was born after the end of the First World War, and in his thinking, he focused mainly on the issues of morality, justice, and fairness.

In his writings, Rawls emphasizes that the concept of justice according to which we must act is justice as fairness. Rawls claims that a society should decide in advance what its principles will be and what will be considered just and unjust.

He believed that the decisions regarding those principles of justice should be made at the start. During the formation of the state under a "veil of ignorance."

This is a hypothetical situation where there is equality in the sense that no person is aware of his social position, status, power, or intelligence. Since the choice of the principles of justice is made when no one knows what their situation is socially or economically (behind a veil of ignorance), it can be said that the principles are the result of a fair deal because they were chosen when no one knew which principle might benefit him and which might harm him.

The constitution, laws, institutions, bodies and authorities that will be established in any society will be based on the principles of justice that were agreed upon in the initial state. Rawls produces a theory that is built on a kind of imaginary social experiment, wherein in a hypothetical situation, a group of people is put in a room without knowing anything about their lives, from the amount of money they have in their bank account to their family status, their place of residence, their life circumstances, their talents and shortcomings.

Precisely in this state of ignorance, Rawls claims that people will choose guiding rules and principles regarding their lives and regarding the society in which they want to live, and those rules and principles will be fair. This is because they were chosen by a group of people who are unaware of their status and have no personal interests. This group is made up of individuals who do not know what will benefit them personally (because they are under a veil of ignorance) and will, therefore, choose the option that benefits the group as a whole.

Rawls does not deny the fact that each person is born into different life circumstances that affect his chances. Still, he believes that a society operating according to the concept will be the closest to a voluntary plan. Nonetheless, he believes that a society functioning under this concept would closely resemble a voluntary system. He explains that although the concepts of justice and fairness are not the same, the term "justice as fairness" expresses the idea that consent was given to the principles of justice in the initial state, which is a fair state and therefore, the principles themselves are the result of a fair transaction, principles that (in some hypothetical situation) free and equal people would agree to.

However, isn't Rawls's theory a misrepresentation?

After all, we do not live in some hypothetical world but in a grounded reality where every person, society, or country prioritizes their private interests over those of society as a whole.

Be that as it may, Rawls does not deny the fact that people are born into different life circumstances. From this, it can be concluded that countries also arise, exist, and are conducted according to their various circumstances.

Since the events of October 7th, actually, since the beginning of the war, the State of Israel has been under intense and continuous international criticism for its activities in the Gaza Strip and in general. The "political hourglass" is a term that Israeli society often uses, and this is due to the repeated accusations by the leaders of various countries and various international organizations about the way that the State of Israel conducts itself in general and the Israel Defense Forces in particular within the Gaza Strip.

Many of the criticisms include the claim that since Israel is the stronger party in the war, meaning the one with the most military capability, it is also more responsible for what is happening.

Other criticisms increasingly blame Israel simply for the dismal civil situation of the residents of the Gaza Strip.

Others believe that Israel is a country that does not choose peace and brotherhood, and proof of this is the large number of wars and operations in which it has participated.

Returning to Rawls and trying to give answers to the criticism: I believe that in some hypothetical situation, one in which the State of Israel is not bombarded, targeted and threatened by its neighbors, a situation in which terrorists do not break into its territory and murder, rape, burn and loot its citizens, the State of Israel would indeed not have such a significant number of armed struggles.

But since we are not in such a utopian state, perhaps similar to what Rawls tried to present in his philosophy, Israel is forced to participate in those wars out of necessity.

I personally support, as Rawls also believed, the claim that people are born into different life circumstances—in our case, countries and territories—because this is not a utopian world.

Therefore, the fact that the residents of the Gaza Strip have, perhaps, fallen into a more difficult life due to the humanitarian situation in the Strip (which it is essential to note, was caused first and foremost by the Hamas organization's choice to keep terrorizing the State of Israel at the expense of improving the situation of the residents of the Strip), does not contradict the fact that the IDF is the most humanitarian army in the world, again, considering the circumstances.

That is, if the State of Israel tries to get into Rawls's mindset, into the same veil of ignorance, it would indeed choose principles that do not include weapons, fighter jets, armies, and violence. But since we do not live in the same imaginary veil of ignorance and a utopian and unconfusing world but in a world where cruelty knows no bounds (and we witnessed this on that Black Sabbath), it can be concluded that the State of Israel has not only the right, but also the duty to protect itself and its citizens from its enemies, and will continue to do so without it being wrong.

If there is one thing I heard throughout the testimonies with the survivors of the Nova Festival, the party held near Kibbutz Ra'im on October 7th, 2023, it was probably the best party they had attended in their lives.

"I've been in the rave scene since I was little. I've been going to parties since I was sixteen. I've never seen such a high-quality party in my life, even though I was in South America," **Yaniv Ben Haim**, a twenty-four-year-old from Holon, told me. "Endless smiles, good atmosphere, angelic people, everyone was dressed nicely, everyone knew in advance that it would be a great party with crazy production. You walk around and feel like they put in an effort with money and vibes. Everything was organized and managed."

Reli Azulay, a twenty-five-year-old from Yokneam, also told me about the high quality of that party.

"I generally like nature raves and attend one every few months. Until the moment it all started, it was the best party I've ever been to. I've been to many places, including South America, and it was the best party I've ever attended."

Yonatan Cohen, a twenty-seven-year-old from the South, also testified, "It was a perfect party. Everything was crazy."

So how did the massive party become the biggest and deadliest massacre in the history of the State of Israel and one of the biggest terrorist attacks that history has known?

This is what they went through in the location.

Yaniv Ben Haim

"A friend called me crying and said there were terrorists near him. In the background, I heard a bunch of shots, and the call was cut off. Since then, he has stopped answering the phone."

I started the conversation with Yaniv Ben Haim, a talented twenty-four-year-old travel agent from Holon, on a good note.

"So, when will the good old days return, when will the war be over, and will I be able to book some tickets abroad from you?" I asked with a smile.

But Yaniv still hasn't recovered from what he witnessed at the horrific party, even though over two months have passed.

"I haven't returned to normal yet. There's nothing I can do about it," he told me, "To this day, I still can't sleep."

I asked him why they decided to attend the party in the first place.

"Just before I and nine friends decided to travel to South America, we found out that one of us had cancer. That friend decided to join us on the trip even though he found out about the disease. We were at a crazy party in Brazil, and when we heard that the same one was being brought to Israel, we had no doubt that we would go to it together as well," he said with a faint smile and continued. "So, we arrived at the party in Israel around midnight, as soon as it started. We were nine of the ten friends that flew together. Only one of us, the guy who has cancer, was delayed and was supposed to arrive in the morning," said Yaniv while praising the quality of the party. Yaniv noted that he and his friends brought alcohol in advance, knowing that drinking at the party would be expensive. "Of course, they didn't let us bring in the vodka, so when we wanted to drink more, we simply left the party, went to the car, and then went back inside. At about 6:15 a.m., we made the trip from the car to the party again. We must have drunk about four liters of vodka that night. We danced like crazy; it was sunrise, and everyone was in a crazed state. About fifteen minutes later, the DJ suddenly stopped the music. We didn't understand why at that moment - because we didn't hear alarms or anything like that. He said there was a 'Red Alert,' and some of us also managed to hear the explosions in the sky," said Yaniv, who was obviously intoxicated at this point in the party.

He continued, "The police officers, who weren't in large numbers at all, took us out to the parking lot and told us to lie on the ground. The police officers kept directing us where to go and what to do, but I wasn't stressed at all at those moments. Those were only alarms. What could happen? It was all good. Also, the police officers were calm; they understood it was a 'Red Alert' and that we just had to duck to protect ourselves until the alarms went off. No one was truly worried."

I asked Yaniv when it was decided to wrap up the party, which was supposed to continue until midday that day.

"Towards 8:00 a.m., we already began to realize that there were many alerts. Although we were not afraid, the police decided to open a road to allow the revelers to return to their homes. There was one road heading left towards Be'eri via Road 232 and one heading right towards Kibbutz Re'im. At this point, my friends and I decided to stay at the party while hundreds of revelers decided to leave. In retrospect, I know that almost everyone who ran away in the first 'batch' - was murdered."

"Then why did you actually decide to stay at the party and not leave at the first opportunity you were given?" I asked Yaniv, who immediately mentioned his friend with cancer.

"So, that friend was supposed to arrive at the party at those very moments. At approximately 7:30 a.m., he sent me a message and told me that he was in a 'Migunit' near Kibbutz Mefalsim and that there were a lot of terrorists outside in the area. He ordered us not to leave the party area." Yaniv said that he was skeptical about what his friend told him and even laughed about it, "I sent him a picture of all the friends from the party and wrote, 'Everything is good, bro. What's wrong with you? What terrorists?'"

That friend with cancer did not hesitate to call his friend.

"I'm in a 'Migunit' in Mefalsim, and there are terrorists here, but everything is fine," he told Yaniv in the phone call. Yaniv said that suddenly, he started hearing screams in Arabic in the background of the conversation and did not understand what was happening.

"Then I heard gunshots. I also heard his cries. Then the call was cut off," he said, adding, "I continued to call him after that, but he no longer answered."

He said that the father and mother of that friend with cancer called him as well because their son did not answer them. They screamed on the phone to get every piece of information, but Yaniv had no answers.

"My mother begged me to run for her. She didn't stop screaming. I told her I loved her - and hung up."

"At that point, we already realized that we had to find a way out, and we were standing in the traffic jam on one of the roads leaving the party. We were in one of the last cars in the traffic jam," Yaniv said. "The police were the ones who led the convoy on the highway, and when there were alarms, we got out of the cars and hid under the bridge that was in the party area. In one of the alarms, I found a young woman who looked very scared; I tried to help her. Now I know she was eventually murdered."

Yaniv said that all this time, they continued to wait in traffic inside the car, trying to get out of the party through the road opened by the police, but the traffic did not move forward.

"Suddenly, right in front of the policemen that were at the beginning of the traffic jam, some pickup trucks pulled over. Three pickup trucks with ATVs on them. All the trucks were full of people holding submachine guns, and I started hearing explosions. No one understood what it was about or who was in these trucks. Some people ran in the direction of the trucks, trying to understand what was happening."

In one moment, he said, the police started screaming at the passengers in the convoy to get out of the cars immediately, turn to the side, and run no matter where, just start running and escape.

I tried to find out what the policemen meant by simply running. Did they give any direction?

Yaniv replied, "Just as I've told you. They screamed to run and escape, no matter where to. Just run as fast as possible."

Yaniv told me about the first incident he was exposed to when he got out of the car at the police's order.

"I saw eight policemen with drawn pistols who did not stop shooting. Though the trucks were still packed with some submachine guns, there were no longer any people in them. The terrorists had time to get out of the trucks and started shooting everywhere. At that moment, all the police officers fell; they all died on the spot. Only two policemen were still alive, a Jew and an Arab, who also ran out of ammunition, so they just started running away with us."

"Did you even realize at that moment that these were terrorists?" I had to stop him and find out what he felt in those moments.

"No, absolutely not. I didn't understand. I was totally drunk. While we were sitting in the car, we continued to laugh among ourselves and tried to get rid of the buzz from the party," he answered.

"So, where did you run off to?" I asked, trying to understand where he went from there.

"At that moment, everyone ran to another place. There were nine of us friends in two cars, one behind the other in the convoy, and as soon as we were told to run, everyone ran in a different direction. For almost an hour, each of us was alone in another place, in this inferno. Only thanks to another friend of mine who was sitting at home and managed to direct us to meet again - we managed to reunite. Each of us sent the same friend a location in real-time, and that's how he managed to bring us together."

Yaniv said that during this time, the terrorists continued to shoot at them.

"We hid, and they kept shooting in our direction. We hid for a minute or two, and we heard gunshots non-stop. The shots didn't stop for a moment. Then we kept running, hid again on the ground, under various objects, and moved from one place to another. We were hiding and running, running, and hiding all the time. It was like that for nineteen miles. I didn't even know where I was running."

During Yaniv's desperate run to save his life, he experienced moments in one of his hiding spots that would forever be engraved in his memory.

"I remember one moment when I was alone, still without my friends who had separated from me, and I hid in the orchard. It was quiet, and it was a spot where everyone hid under the trees and branches. The terrorists had already reached the orchard on foot because they did not want to fall with their vehicles into the large pits that were near the trees. They were twenty-two yards away from me, and they were shooting everywhere, at any moving target, at any sign of life. Suddenly, out of the corner of my eye, I saw my friend next to me, one of my best friends. After almost an hour of running non-stop, hiding under tarps, hearing gunshots everywhere, I was still drunk when I suddenly saw him. It was an exciting moment. I remember we grabbed each other and hugged so tightly. We almost kissed. That's how thrilled we were. Although we were euphoric, we also understood that it was over. It was almost 8:30 a.m., and I had already managed to see the terrorists everywhere on foot, on motorcycles, on ATVs, and help, of course, did not come. That was the moment we realized it was the end. They were close to us, only a few feet away, and they just kept moving forward. We also had nowhere to run because they surrounded us from all directions. My friend turned to me and whispered so that the terrorists wouldn't hear that he was happy to die with me. I've called my parents via video one last time, and they've heard all the gunshots around us. I could only tell them, 'I love you,' that's all. Immediately after – "I hung up."

I stopped him from talking. "How did your parents react in that conversation?" I asked.

Yaniv told me about their anxiety.

"There were only screams on the phone from their side, only screams. My mom begged me in tears that I would run for her, and my dad screamed at me that I was the only man he had at home, so I must get out of there alive for him, even though I have two other brothers," Yaniv said with a tiny smirk.

"I saw men who had their dicks cut off and put in their mouths."

"We kept hearing the whistles of the gunshots, and we saw the bullets going through the perforated leaves in the plantation. We understood that it was over if we didn't run for our lives. My friends and I started running madly. By a miracle, we were able to move forward unharmed, and on the way, we saw horrors such as people full of blood and bodies on the ground. We saw everything and anything, and the terrorists were all around us. We didn't know where to run," Yaniv said. "Slowly, our group re-gathered and started running together in one direction. The problem was that we didn't know which direction to run to. We understood that, on the one hand, there were terrorists in Be'eri, and on the other hand, there were terrorists in Re'im. They were also coming from the North about twenty-two yards from us, and if we turned left to Netivot and Sderot, there were also terrorists there. Our only option was to run straight towards Moshav Patish, an Israeli village about twenty-five miles from the party area. And that's what we did; we started running, of course, in a zigzag pattern because the terrorists were shooting at us. On the way, we found cover and hiding spots. We laid on the ground, jumped, hid, did everything to stay alive," he said. "During that long run, we also passed through the party area itself," Yaniv said while rolling his eyes. "There, we saw things that are not easy to talk about. Things that are not easy to talk about at all."

Yaniv was silent for a few seconds and continued, "Everything was chaotic. I breathed in the air. I still remember the smell. I saw a body on the ground, and I was still drunk. I couldn't understand why everything looked like that."

Yaniv said that there was a friend next to him who was also still drunk and asked him with incredible innocence about the terrorists, "Tell me, why are they angry with us? Why are they doing this? Let them come dance with us."

I insisted that Yaniv still tell me more of what he witnessed at those moments in the party area, even though I understood the insensitivity of the matter.

"I saw naked girls running away, and that's when they were still alive. I also saw naked girls on the ground, dead. I saw men shot in the head, unrecognizable because of the shot."

Yaniv continued to share about the horrors. "I saw men who had their dicks cut off and put in their mouths. Other people with severed limbs. Hands, fingers, legs, a severed head on the ground on another side altogether. I saw cars burning, people dying inside the cars, and other people, actually corpses, lying outside the cars. Lots of people have been stabbed, and others with all kinds of limbs that are suddenly in a strange position. Suddenly, they don't have an arm or leg, or there is a body without a head. Some bodies exploded; all the organs were thrown in different places. Imagine a brain that explodes – that's what I saw there."

"Naked girls ran everywhere. One of them shit on herself out of fear."

I tried to ask Yaniv about the naked girls he saw at the party area to understand their condition. If they had been raped, I wanted to know how they managed to stay alive.

Yaniv replied, "There were naked girls who ran with me. Some men took off their clothes to bring them to them. To answer your question, those women did not take off their clothes, but the terrorists took them off of them. They managed to escape amidst all the chaos that took place there."

Yaniv did not skimp on the details and shared what he had witnessed.

"A girl was standing in front of me. She was completely naked, all covered in her own shit. She bent down on the ground and shit on herself out of fear. And we kept running into the forest, into the field," Yaniv said as if he was in pain, "It was so dam hot, and we had a liter and a half of water that had to be divided among ten people. One was dehydrated, the other stoned, the third drunk, the fourth confused. On the way, when we ran, we looked for water on people's bodies. One of my friends threw up seven or more times; we didn't know what to do with him. There was a stage where my friend and I carried him in our arms. And that's how we kept running, ten friends in an open field from plantation to plantation, long and tedious miles, knowing that if we stopped, there would be no going back. When possible, we hide. When we heard shots, we ran."

But this story had a happy ending, and Yaniv said, "One of my good friends is the nephew of the Israeli singer Lior Narkis. Although the vast majority of us no longer had a battery on our phones at this point, the singer somehow managed to call his nephew. He was frightened by the gunshots in the background and said he'd send someone to rescue us. We, who were under attack, realized that no one could really come and save us, and we kept running until we reached a safe place, a farm nearby. We also found a water cooler there, which was a miracle for us. We drank non-stop."

Despite the doubts, the singer, Lior Narkis, managed to call a rescuer.

"He called and said he would arrange for someone to pick us up, but he warned in advance that we would have to trust him even though he is Arab," Yaniv said.

Indeed, the person who came to save Yaniv and his friends was an Arab-Israeli citizen named Ibrahim. He went to the party area in his private car and, for hours, managed to save people from the inferno. He put everyone he could in his vehicle but waited exclusively for Yaniv and his friends despite the inferno around him.

"We got into the car and left the area of fire. On the way, we saw soldiers, and the same Arab got out of the car and screamed at them that there were dead people in the party," Yaniv said.

In the midst of all this, despite the heroism of that Arab citizen and due to the utterly understandable security circumstances of October 7th, the soldiers who met that citizen took the passengers out of the car and demanded that they raise their hands.

To this, Yaniv said, "We got out of the car and put our hands up. It turns out that the soldiers didn't understand if we were actually kidnapped or not until they realized that the Arab guy was the one who saved us in the first place."

The irony in the situation was that the IDF soldiers got help from that civilian who directed them to where the terrorists were.

"And what about your parents? All this time, they didn't know anything about you? Only that you love them?" I asked Yaniv, who said that by 8:00 a.m., his battery had run out.

"During the run, which lasted long and tiring hours, I stopped people along the way and begged them to lend me a phone."

I asked Yaniv to tell me about the content of his conversations with his parents at that moment.

Yaniv held out his hands to me and shared with me that he felt chills in his body.

"At first, they didn't understand. My sister took the phone away from my mom and told her, 'Calm down, he's an idiot. He must have taken something,' while screaming at me and asking what I took and why I was so stupid to use drugs. I kept claiming that there were terrorists, but they didn't believe me until they heard the shots. Then they understood that there was a mess. I ran in video mode for about half an hour with the phone in my pocket and didn't know what to do. I even turned the screen and filmed the terrorists, the shots, and the RPG for them. My father got frustrated and told me, 'You're in Shuja'iyya, inside Gaza. I don't know how you'll get out of there.' Yaniv also shared what he realized in retrospect, "My mother kicked things in the house and broke her leg. When I returned home, she was the one who had gone to the hospital."

"I lost ten very close friends, good people that will never return."

"And you actually went home that Saturday. What did you do on that day?" I asked Yaniv.

He answered, "I got home, hugged everyone, and cried like a little girl whose pacifier was taken away. My father took all my friends and me straight to the synagogue so that they would give us the 'Birkat Hagomel[1].' In the synagogue, no one understood what happened and what it meant because it was Saturday, and none of those present were connected to the news."

But like every story that happened on October 7th, miracles were accompanied by severe disasters.

"There were twenty of us friends at the party, and about half of them were good and close friends who were together in South America. Only fifty percent of us survived. Ten friends remained alive, and I was among them. Ten were murdered. Some were murdered in containers, some at the party itself, some ran away from the party to Kibbutz Be'eri and were murdered there, and some were murdered in the Migunit. We lost ten good people, very close friends, who will not return."

Yaniv said that the first week after the attack was a week dedicated only to funerals, one after another. "Already on Saturday, we started receiving the news about our friends who were murdered. The following week, we had to go to their funerals. On average, we had more than one funeral a day."

I asked Yaniv how he has dealt with the situation since then.

---

1. It is a blessing of praise to God for a favor He has bestowed on the blesser, was in a danger of losing his life or faced some other significant threat was saved from it.

"With a lot, a lot of weeds. It calms the dreams at night. In the middle of the day, it sometimes stops me from thinking. On top of that, a lot of psychological treatments. I'm just waiting for it to pass. Until the war is over, I won't get over it. I still dream that I'm running, that I'm being chased, I hear the shots, I smell the smell," Yaniv said.

I asked him what had happened to his personal belongings, which he had left at the party and maybe in his car.

"Everything was left there: the headphones, the charger, the money, the wallet, the car. The car, of course, is no longer drivable. It's filled with bullet holes and burned. They didn't tell me exactly what was in it. I do know that it probably had DNA from people who were murdered. Everything was taken away. By the way, if I go back to those moments under attack, I remember being so drunk that in those moments, even though I was sure I was going to die, I turned to a friend who was next to me and said to him, 'Bro, you left two thousand shekels in your wallet. They are in my car.' He cursed me jokingly, as his last words."

To sum this story up, I asked Yaniv how he felt at the funeral of his friend who had cancer and was murdered in the Migunit in Mefalsim while warning him about the terrorists.

I must admit, I did not expect Yaniv's answer at all.

"That friend with cancer survived. The terrorists threw a grenade into the Migunit and shot him twice, two bullets. Up until two weeks ago, he was declared to be in level 8 at the hospital, mortally wounded, and this is in addition to cancer he is battling. He survived, and today, he is no longer at the hospital. This is one of my best friends. I grew up with him almost since birth. And yes, this is also his story."

"So, how do you feel now, Yaniv?" I tried to find out about his feelings after the conversation.

Yaniv took a deep breath and answered honestly, "I won't lie. My hands are sweaty."

Although I tried to encourage him, deep in my heart, I knew this was another victim of the Black Sabbath. Another victim, albeit a hero, but still a kid. A kid who saw the worst of all.

Reli Azoulay

"The road was filled with bodies. The terrorists saw us. From that moment, it was just chaos."

Reli Azulay, a twenty-five-year-old from Yokneam, a city in the Northern Region of Israel, is a former IDF fighter and currently studies Pilates as part of a professional course.

Until that party, she also had a routine with a regular job.

"I've pushed everyone away. I still don't sleep at all. I'm so tired all the time. I started driving again a month after the incident out of fear that I would be shot and wouldn't be able to control the car. It was only two weeks ago that I even managed to return to Pilates studies," she said painfully.

"Why did you even decide to go to that party?" I asked Reli, who smiled and said that she really likes nature and rave parties and even that she and her friends go to a massive party of this kind every few months.

"I bought a ticket to the party along with some girlfriends five months before it took place. Everything was planned precisely. My partner, Eden, and his friends also bought tickets to the party. We drove there in three cars. I was with my partner and his friends. We arrived at the party around 2:00 a.m., set up the friend's tent, and smuggled drinks. We started drinking some alcohol, Arak[2], went to the dance floor and started having fun. It was an amazing party. At around 6:30 a.m., we started to hear some strange noise. At first, I thought it was a problem with the speakers, but then the

---

2.   A distilled Levantine spirit of the anise drinks family.

DJ stopped the music, announced that there was a 'Red Alert' and ordered everyone to evacuate the dance floor," Reli said.

In those very moments, Reli's nightmare began.

"We went towards the exit and threw ourselves on the ground to protect ourselves from the missiles. At around 7:00 a.m., when they began to understand the magnitude of the situation, they told us to pack our things and evacuate the party. We started to pack our things, but only what was necessary. We tried to reach our cars as quickly as possible, but finding them took us a long time."

Reli said that when they managed to get to the cars, they were among the first to leave the party, in fact, in the first convoy.

"At about 7:20 a.m., we managed to get out of the traffic jam that had formed on the road and turned right in the direction of a Migunit in Re'im. Eden and his friends were in the car. We were very calm; we smoked cigarettes in the car and continued to listen to songs. We knew that in the Migunit, we would be safe."

The Migunit that Reli is talking about is the same Migunit that later became a death trap for all the partygoers who were brutally slaughtered by Hamas's terrorists.

Reli continued, "We drove for two to three minutes in the direction of Re'im, and then we saw that they just stopped the road, blocked it and surrounded it from all directions. Many bodies were lying on the ground, and we had to stop the vehicle to understand what was happening. At first, we didn't realize what it was; we didn't know why the other cars were so severely damaged and why there were bodies on the ground.

Eden noticed suspicious movements out of the corner of his eye. Realizing they were probably terrorists, he yelled at his friend (the car's driver) to turn the car around. As soon as he did, the terrorists saw us and picked up on our movement. From that moment, it was pure chaos."

"My father begged me to survive. They made him swallow anti-anxiety pills. The police said we can only pray."

"The terrorists began shooting in all directions at our car, trying to flip it over, just as they had done to the other cars in front of us. The bodies lying on the road ahead were from those overturned cars.

The airbags opened immediately, the tires were punctured, and the car took a brutal hit. In retrospect, when you look at the car today, you see it has bullet holes everywhere. It is not an actual car. There were ten terrorists, and they did not stop shooting. I remember the sounds of the shooting and Eden, my partner, who did not stop screaming. He screamed that they were shooting at the car and begged everyone to duck," Reli recounted.

I immediately had to find out how she felt during those moments.

"The truth is that I froze. I ducked, but I didn't understand what was happening. I'm from the North; I barely know what 'Red Alerts' are and certainly not what terrorists are. Although I was a soldier, I was never in a situation where I had no way to defend myself," she said.

Reli recounted that despite the heavy fire towards the car, they managed to drive back towards the party.

"I don't know how we managed to continue driving in the state the car was in, but we got back to the party area because there was nowhere else to go since the terrorists had surrounded the entire area deliberately so as not to allow anyone to leave."

Indeed, they initially deliberately made the dance floor into a slaughterhouse, which unfortunately succeeded in part.

The moment Reli, Eden, and their friends returned to the party area, they called the police and screamed for help, but the answer they got on that phone call emphasized the depth of the chaos.

"They just told us they knew and that we needed to pray, and it would be okay. They said they could do nothing to help," Reli recounted. "So, we left the car and left everything there, water, shoes, clothes, bags, everything, and we started running," she continued, "It was a run for our lives. At first, we joined my girlfriends, with whom I came to the party, but the terrorists were behind us, and my girlfriends ran faster than us, advanced, and we lost them. Meanwhile, I was still with my boyfriend and his friends, running through the orchards between the big holes and trees. Everywhere we ran to, they ran after us. It was like that for several hours. We hid to survive."

"Where did you go from there?" I asked Reli to tell me about the continuation of the horrific journey.

"At around 11:00 a.m., we arrived at an area with clementine orchards and hid there. The orchards were between Re'im and Urim, in the middle of the war zone. When we were there, my parents found out where I was. Until then, they didn't even know what was going on."

I asked Reli why she hadn't contacted them until then, and she replied, "On the first calls to the police, they promised us that they would arrive soon, so I wanted to update my parents only after everything was okay. The answer was completely different on later calls, so I didn't want to worry them."

"So, what did you talk about on that phone call while you were hiding in the orchards and when terrorists were running around you?" I asked Reli.

She replied, "My father asked me where I was, and I told him that I was hiding in the field. He didn't understand. He didn't stop sending me voice messages in which he screamed that he was dying many times and that I needed to tell him where I was. He was stressed. He wanted to come and rescue us, but we told him that if he did, he would probably die on the way. Even while we were hiding in the orchards, we continued to hear the shootings everywhere," Reli recounted. "At around 12:00 p.m. I already understood that no one would rescue us, and the terrorists were too close. I wrote to my father that I love him and the whole family and told Eden I love him too. It was important to me that they know."

I insisted on hearing from Reli what her father had responded to that "last message" that was sent to him.

Reli told me that he begged her not to do this to him and again noted that he felt he was about to die. "In retrospect, I know that he almost had a heart attack at home. My mother told me that later. She told me that she had to put anti-anxiety pills into his mouth to calm him down."

"We didn't intend to save you either, so be thankful."

Reli said that when they hid in the orchards, every time they heard gunshots, they moved to hide in another tree so as not to become stationary targets.

"The hiding places were actually trees with a lot of leaves. We climbed it and stayed inside. We were in complete silence. We couldn't even move because there were many branches, and we made noise as soon as we moved. So, we just tried to be frozen and in silence. At one point, we caught sight of an Israeli vehicle with a driver and two wounded people in the back. The three got out of the car and joined us in the hideout. One of them got a bullet in the throat and died next to us. He just crashed in the orchards. The other, who was wounded in the leg, laid on the grass comfortably and smoked a cigarette as if it was the 'last cigarette,'" she said.

Reli told me that at this point, while hiding in the orchards, they called the police again because they believed that this time, they would come to rescue them, now that they were with a person who had a gunshot wound which needed urgent treatment, but this did not happen.

"At around 2:00 p.m., a vehicle arrived at the orchards area. At first, we ran away from it because we thought they were terrorists. While we were hiding from the vehicle, we heard voices in Hebrew and realized that they were Israelis. We didn't leave the driver much choice. All five of us crammed into the trunk and informed him that we would not leave," Reli said.

They drove in the trunk to the gas station in Urim, where they waited another hour while continuing to be exposed to the horrors.

"We saw a lot of bodies at the gas station as well; there were a lot of injured people. I don't even know what happened to them. At one point, an officer came to refuel his car, and we begged him to take us with him. The officer was convinced and drove us to the Ofakim police station," she said.

When they arrived at the police station in Ofakim, they asked to go inside because there were also a large number of terrorists in Ofakim, but the police refused to let them in.

"They just left us out," Reli said. "I went to the police officer at the front desk and told her about other friends of mine who were under attack and needed immediate help and rescue. I also provided her with their whereabouts."

She did not expect the answer she received from that woman.

"There's nothing to do; it's a war zone; let them pray - we didn't intend to save you either, so be thankful. A freak coincidence saved you," the officer scolded her.

Only in the end, when there were warnings of terrorist infiltration in Ofakim, and the police realized that it was not safe to leave the young people outside, they finally let them inside the station.

"Also, in Ofakim, there were a lot of 'Red Alerts,' and you have ten seconds to enter the safe room. At that time, we were sitting in the police station along with the terrorists caught by the police," Reli said. "At this point, we still had no food, but at least we had some water. We were at the police station until about 8:00 p.m."

"The bodies were limp, thrown and broken. It was difficult to recognize that they were human beings."

In the evening, Reli and her friends managed to get a ride back home. They went to her partner's house in Netanya, where her father was waiting for her, to bring her back to Yokneam.

"Eden and I have been together for over a year, and when we arrived in Netanya, it was the first time my father and my boyfriend's father had met. It's unbelievable that it happened under these circumstances. My partner's parents and my family were waiting for us in a line, and everyone was crying. It was a bizarre situation. No one could ever even imagine such a situation," Reli said, awkwardly describing the first and somewhat out-of-the-ordinary time that the couple's families met.

"My mother says that when I came home, my gaze was frozen; it was dead - the gaze of someone who had seen corpses. And I did see corpses," Reli said.

I asked her about the condition of those corpses she had seen.

"As they were shooting at us, I saw the bodies that were thrown out of other vehicles. They were on the ground, limp, thrown, broken. At first, I didn't even realize those were bodies because they didn't look like bodies. They were so broken and disfigured, so how could I know that it was a body at all? How can it be a human being? They looked like the most illogical way a human body can be. During the run, I saw people falling next to me and beside me, throwing things to make it easier for them to run - total chaos. I didn't know whether to stop and help those people or to keep running for my life. I didn't know whether to try to call the police again or stop, make a video, and start documenting what was happening," she shared.

"I assume you were still kind of drunk at this point?" I asked Reli, who nodded her head.

"You are in an unusual situation that is not normal, so you have no choice. I remember that I felt like I was tasting metal due to the long run without water, and this is also because I drank alcoholic drinks earlier, which added to the difficulty."

I asked Reli if she believed that she'd get out of the situation alive.

"No, I didn't believe I'd get out of there. In the orchards, I really thought this was it; it was over. I heard the terrorists getting closer; I heard the shots getting louder and louder. I heard it coming, and I realized that this was the end, that this was the last stage. So, admittedly, I didn't think I would get out of it, but my partner Eden did believe. He kept saying that we would get out of this alive."

"And how do you feel about the treatment you received from the police, and in general, about the fact that for hours there was no army, no rescue forces, and people were slaughtered with no one there to help them?" I asked Reli, who honestly tried to call for help many times but never succeeded.

"It's abandonment. That day, I was very angry with the state and the army. In retrospect, I still think it's abandonment, but also that it's something much bigger than us, than Israel. I think we were just pawns in something much bigger than us. Am I angry? Of course. The army observers' alerts simply stopped. Because they knew, and they knew months in advance, and it wasn't just one person who alerted, but somewhere in the reporting chain, it stopped, and they abandoned us," Reli claimed.

Regarding the treatment she received from the police, she said, "At the time, I was furious, but in retrospect, I understand that they were also in chaos. They also didn't know what to do, and the first police officers who went out to rescue people from the party were also murdered. And yet, although I'm not judging, they weren't the nicest. They were not so sympathetic to the situation we came out of and the situation we were in. Yes, it was terrible."

Reli said that she lost many friends. "Mostly people I knew from South America, a lot of acquaintances were also injured. Fortunately, the friends who came with me to the party, the same friends we lost along the way, survived."

And I just wondered to myself what would have happened if Reli, Eden and their friends had managed to escape the terrorists on the road and reach the Migunit in Re'im? I realized that if that had happened, this conversation would not have taken place at all, and these words would not have been written.

Stories of this kind that Reli experienced are not easily defined as miracles. Nevertheless, the nightmares are still here, and the anxieties will probably not go away anytime soon.

And yet, they are here with us. Living, breathing, and loving, and for that, we can only say thank God.

Yonatan Cohen

"In our case, there were early signs. We felt that something bad was about to happen."

Yonatan Cohen, a twenty-seven-year-old electrical engineer from the Shoham area, has not returned to work since the massacre at the party.

"But I also freelance in the field of music. I write, compose, and sing," said Yonatan, who also shared the reason why he came to the party in the first place. "When I'm alone, I don't even listen to trance music, but when I go out to a party, it's only for a rave party. It sounds strange, but it's mainly because of the atmosphere, the friends, and everything is more fun there. There is this kind of authenticity, a kind of freedom." Yonatan continued, "But I wasn't supposed to attend this party. I didn't even have a ticket. A week before the event, I met with a good friend of mine, and she drove me crazy, asking me to go with her and her cousin. Only then was I convinced."

Indeed, he purchased a ticket to the party following his girlfriend's request. That friend, along with her cousin, were murdered by Hamas terrorists at the festival.

As he lit a cigarette, Yonatan shared with me what he called the "preliminaries" of the massacre. According to him, those who appeared before he arrived at the party warned him of what would happen.

"There were five of us, including me, two friends and two other girlfriends, were in the car going to the party. It was my private car, and I was the driver. Just before we left, on the way to my house, those girlfriends called me and told me they had an accident and that the whole car was dismantled. They told me with a slight laugh that the event does not bode well for the rest of the day, but I told them not to worry."

A few moments before Yonatan and his friends set off, his sister-in-law arrived at his house.

"She asked us not to go. She said that the party was in the South, right next to the border's fence, and there might be missiles, and that it was dangerous. I told her that everything would be fine and that we were all going to the party, and we set off. When we stopped at a gas station to get ice for the drinks, we saw a sticker stuck on one of the machines. It said, 'You'll regret this.' One of the friends, Nicole, told us that she had a bad feeling, that it was a bad sign and that something bad was going to happen at the party," Yonatan said.

"Come with no expectations, and it will be 'totally awesome,'" Niv said, one of our friends, in response to Nicole's concerns.

Yonatan also said that on the way to the party, the group listened to the songs played on the radio because they wanted to save battery on their phones, and the songs, according to him, were all sad and depressing.

"Some were shot in the hand; some had bullets in their stomachs. It was sickening."

"At about 2:00 a.m., we arrived at the party that was supposed to end mid-day the next day. We parked the car closest to the Gaza Strip fence. We got in and started having fun; it was perfect. At about 6:30 a.m., the alarms and rockets started, and some chaos erupted all around us. Some people were very stressed and started running everywhere; some girls screamed, others lay down on the ground, but we didn't panic. We had already assessed that, for security reasons, the party would not continue; we packed our things and walked towards the car," Yonatan said.

"At this point, were you still high? From alcohol, maybe drugs too?" I asked Yonatan.

He replied, "Yes, that was the stage when everyone was at their peak, during the sunrise. I was high, too."

Yonatan told me about the vast number of rockets he saw up in the air.

"There were rockets in abnormal amounts. Some rockets just passed over us. The whole sky was filled with rockets. There were also some paragliders that passed over us; at that stage, we thought it was the residents of the South who were having fun," he said. When in fact, in retrospect, Yonatan was referring to the paragliders that helped the Hamas terrorists infiltrate into Israeli territory on the morning of October 7th.

"So, at around 7:00 a.m. I, along with my friends Gilad and Niv and my girlfriends Meitar and Nicole, walked towards the car while, in the background, the police already informed us to leave the party area. We got to the car, and I tried to start it, but even after several attempts, the car simply did not respond; the brakes and steering wheel were locked. My friend, Meitar, was stressed and urged me to continue and try to fix the problem, but I stepped out of the car to smoke a cigarette and wait for something to change. At the time, I did not understand at all the magnitude of the incident or what it was about," Yonatan shared.

But for Yonatan and his friends, the event was far from over.

"We started hearing gunshots, but they were far away from us. We thought it was probably a wedding or that it was a routine shooting by Gaza Division soldiers near the border fence. In retrospect, it was probably the shooting that took place at Kibbutz Be'eri and Kibbitz Re'im, which were not far away from us. At the same time, a friend who had already left the party called me and begged me not to leave the area and that there were terrorists everywhere. I didn't listen to her. I was so high. I told her she was imagining it."

After about ten minutes, Yonatan tried to start the car again and succeeded. He and his friends got into the car and started driving toward the exit, but they got stuck in a traffic jam that created a bottleneck.

"My friends pressured me to drive around the traffic jam like many others did, but I refused and stayed in line. We continued to drive slowly in the traffic jam until we reached a police blockade at the entrance to the Be'eri and Ra'im area," he said.

Miraculously, the car in front of him, with three people in it, was the last one allowed to enter the kibbutzim, and immediately after it entered, the police decided to block the entry.

"There is no access, the police told me and implored me to turn back despite the long traffic jam we were already in and needed to return home. We were the next car in line that was supposed to enter the kibbutzim, and the police ordered us to return to the party area," he said.

I needed to understand the chain of events that caused the miracles that happened and prevented him from entering the inferno that occurred in the kibbutzim.

"So actually, the car not responding and delaying you, and the fact that you decided not to bypass the other vehicles in the traffic jam despite pressure from your friends, and the fact that you were the first car that the police did not let in saved you?" I asked Yonatan, knowing that most of the partygoers who were the first to leave and flee to the kibbutzim did not return.

"Yes. In retrospect, if I had been one car in front of me, we would probably all have died. We would have entered one of the 'shelters from hell' and exploded there, just like what happened to the car in front of us where one of the passengers was murdered, and two lost their legs while hiding in the Migunit when grenades were thrown at them by the terrorists. Yonatan continued, "The malfunction of the car, the fact that it didn't start, probably because of the battery, saved us for sure. Even today, when I replay in my mind what happened and imagine that if the car had started on the first try, I know for sure that there is no way I would have survived. Either I would have exploded in the Migunit, or I would have been murdered inside the kibbutzim or outside. The car's malfunction saved my life."

Yonatan told me he visited two of the car's three passengers who drove in front of him at the rehabilitation center. They were alive even though their legs were amputated.

This is the car that still managed to exit the party area just before the police blocked the exit for Yonatan and his friends. "I told them I was in the car behind them," Yonatan said of the exciting and unusual meeting.

While I comprehended that one less car in the traffic jam, or a few seconds, would have prevented me from writing these words, Yonatan continued the story about the inferno that was far from over.

"While the police surrounded us and all the traffic behind us, the shots sounded closer and closer. The terrorists actually closed in on us from Re'im and Be'eri and also from the border fence of the Strip. We had no choice but to abandon the car and flee on foot towards the open areas, where we hid in big pits and holes in the ground."

But the shots only got closer and closer, and Yonatan refused to stay in the pit without knowing what was happening outside.

"I had to find out what it was all about, so I headed back to the road where the cars were left, to the police blockade area. As I was walking there, I started to see people running in the opposite direction, precisely in my direction. People with bullet holes in their bodies. Some were shot in the hand, some with bullets in the stomach. They ran in my direction, bleeding and injured and screaming at me to turn to the other side; it was sickening. That's when I began to understand that this was something that had never been seen before," he said.

"I'm lying in a pit, and bodies are falling on me from above. It was chaos, and people were dropping like flies."

After those sights, Yonatan realized that the escape route must be recalculated.

"We left the pits and started running in an open area towards the east. After we ran a third of a mile, we heard silence and interpreted it as a pause in the shooting or the death of the terrorists. In fact, the terrorists murdered everyone, and no shots were heard for a few minutes. We left the girls to hide in an open area, and again, I went with my friend Niv towards the road for the third time to get the car."

Yonatan said that since everyone was running in the opposite direction, they were the only ones trying to reach the road, so the terrorists aimed only at them.

"They shot specifically at us. We were the only ones there. They shot at us as if we were sitting ducks. We ran, lay down, got up, fell, and hid until we got to the cars. The sights were horrifying. Everyone was dead. The policemen were dead, as well as the IDF soldiers and the few security forces that came to aid. The revelers from the party were also dead, inside and outside the vehicles. It was total chaos. We managed to find the car and drove it to pick up the girls from the open area, but by the time we got there too, a traffic jam had already formed and leaving the party area was impossible."

Yonatan noted that in that traffic jam, cars crashed into each other, and people ran over each other. He said that men screamed, girls fainted, the traffic did not move forward, and people started getting out of their cars while the terrorists approached the area in pickup trucks with different and varied weapons and started shooting everywhere.

"So, we decided to abandon the car and flee on foot again," Yonatan said with desperation in his voice, "there were about five hundred people who left the vehicles and ran in the open. The terrorists were already right next to us. They had two pickup trucks, and in each of them, at least eight terrorists with countless weapons. The terrorists shot everywhere indiscriminately at those five hundred people, and I was one of them. I ran, and people fell next to me. Whoever was hit by a bullet fell, and whoever was not continued running. The bullets passed by our heads, by our bodies, and people dropped like flies. It was like a shooting range, and people were slaughtered."

Yonatan realized that he was targeted at that range and that even if he ran in a zigzag, he could still rely on luck, so he chose a different strategy.

"At this point, my friends and I were already split up. Everyone ran in a different direction; we couldn't stay together. I understood that if I kept running, I would be the next to be hit, so instead, I decided to jump into a huge pit in the ground right in the middle of the area where hundreds of people were still running. I jumped and hid inside. I really hoped that the terrorists wouldn't find me there," he said. " While I was hiding in that pit, lying down, and waiting, the bodies of people shot by the terrorists fell on me from above. I lay there as people ran over me; some continued running, while others fell in—alive, wounded, or dead. I kept lying still, trying not to move so I wouldn't become a target. I was just lying there, waiting for death. The terrorists were about a hundred and ten yards away, shooting everyone and getting closer. I was sure they would see me and shoot me to confirm the kill. But I had no choice but to wait. I had to stay in that pit next to the dead, wounded, and barely living people. Some girls, overcome by fear or exhaustion, fainted and fell into the pit as well."

At first, when he told me about the chaos where hundreds of people ran, and some died at the hands of Hamas terrorists, I pictured in my head the game "Statues" (red light, green light) from the series "Squid Game." The connotation that occurred to me is admittedly childish. Still, it accurately describes what happened, except for one detail: it was not a fictional series but a painful and cruel reality.

When Yonatan continued to tell me about that pit in the ground where he lay with all the bodies, wounded, or living people who tried to hide from the terrorists, the association changed and went from a TV series to the same sights I was exposed to in Poland, specifically the death pits and the ditches of those murdered in the Holocaust. It sounded like Yonatan's descriptions were horrifyingly identical to testimonies from the Second World War, where Jews were massacred by gunfire and fell into the death pits. Some of them pretended to be dead next to the bodies of their relatives so that the Nazis would not kill them.

For a moment, it seemed to me that eighty-four years after that cursed war, the pits of death had "come to life," as ironic as the image may be.

However, there are two main differences between those events: one is dramatic, and the other is a little less so.

The first one is that this time the killers were not German Nazis but the Nazis of the new era, the damned Hamas terrorists.

The second is a more significant difference: this time, the death pits were used again while the Jews had a state of their own, which was independent, sovereign, and strong.

These pits were used in the territory of that state, the state of the Jews, which was established first and foremost to keep them safe and promise that there would never be a second holocaust. Ultimately, the promise was broken.

"I was sure that the whole country was conquered. We thought about how to get to the border in order to escape abroad."

"While I was in that pit, I called my brother and said goodbye to him. 'They are not prepared for anything; there are dead people here. It's chaos,'" Yonatan told his brother. "I told him that I was being shot at. It was moments before death, and I asked him to tell everyone that I loved them, including my parents, who were abroad and didn't know that something was even happening. I even said goodbye to myself. My brother ordered me not to say that and told me that everything would be okay," Yonatan said.

Although he said goodbye to his family, he knew deep down that he would not die.

"I'm the most cowardly and anxious person in the world. I'm not cool and relaxed, and I panic easily. I'm no hero. That's why I'm surprised that I survived it. At that time, in the pit, I was scared to death, but inside, I knew I would survive. I don't know how to explain it, but I didn't feel that it was the end of me. It was an inner feeling of survival."

After spending a long time in the pit, Yonatan decided it was time to get out of it and check what was happening outside.

"The herd of escapees continued to move in my direction. Hundreds of people were still running for their lives. I was the only one who looked in the opposite direction, right at the terrorists. It looked like a movie. The two trucks continued to move with the terrorists on them and continued to shoot indiscriminately. They got closer and closer. At that moment, I froze. I fell silent. I couldn't move. Suddenly, I felt quiet in my head, and I was somewhere else. You could even say that I imagined something peaceful amid this pile of death. I was lost in my thoughts. And again, like in a movie, the people around me fell to the ground non-stop, shot and wounded, and I just stood in the middle and didn't move. The bullets didn't hit me. Miraculously, nothing happened. To this day, I don't understand it. They were right in front of me and shot other people."

After about twenty seconds of the imaginary peace that Yonatan experienced, he heard a voice in the background.

"One of my friends saw me just standing there. He screamed at me like crazy, and I woke up from the dream I was in," Yonatan said, "In my head, I went back into battle mode. I started running in the correct direction, along with other escapees, until I reached an orchard. There, I saw a policeman who couldn't help anyone because he was in the same situation and had no way to aid. We continued running east, towards the sun, bush to bush, with different groups of people. We saw people hiding in trees and ditches. Some were injured, some got kidnapped right next to us, some got murdered in front of our eyes. Everyone was on their own, and even the policeman we met on the way told us that we had permission to do anything to survive. 'Kill, steal, just live, do everything to get home,' he ordered us," Yonatan said. He compared the chaos to the film 'The Purge,' where there are twenty-four hours every year when there are no laws, and every person is free to do whatever he wants without any prohibition, enforcement, or punishment.

"I also thought only of myself; I stuck to large groups of escapees so that someone else would get shot instead of me."

Yonatan's words emphasized how great the sense of helplessness and uncertainty affected the festival goers.

"At no point did we have the assistance of the army or the police. I was alone. I truly thought that the whole country was conquered. I didn't know what was happening outside. Even when I called the police, who only answered after seventeen minutes, I was told to keep hiding, not to move, and that they had nothing to do. When I wanted to escape to the surrounding communities, I was informed that the terrorists had taken them under control, and the same with military bases. I was sure that this was the case throughout the country. I was so sure that my friends and I discussed the need to find a way to escape from the country. When I saw Gazan citizens in front of me traveling around Israel as if it were their home, what could I think? As far as I was concerned, the country was conquered, so I didn't even aim to get home but to find an exit through the border to another country."

Yonatan said that they ran from orchard to orchard, drank water from sewers, and kept going like that for about nineteen miles, and on their way, saw death everywhere.

"At about 1:00 p.m., when we hid in one of the bushes of the orchards, we heard someone shouting in Hebrew. They were citizens who drove a van and tried to save Israelis. We were skeptical for a moment, but when we saw that others were getting on it and not getting killed, we joined in as well. Even then, the attack did not stop because we were evacuated to Moshav Patish. Still, the terrorists got there too, and from there, we were evacuated to Be'er Sheva, where we were constantly hiding from the missiles and 'Red Alerts' - but the main thing is that we got out of the party area."

"The truth must be told. They conquered us with pickup trucks, flip-flops and bandanas on their heads."

Yonatan recounted the first evening when he returned to the Tel Aviv area.

"People were walking normally, and I didn't understand why. How is this place not conquered? Why isn't everyone pulling out weapons? Why do the people here walk around and do nothing? In my head, I was still in a state of battle."

I asked Yonatan about his friends who were murdered and if he was aware of the circumstances of their murder.

"Regarding the people who were in the car with me, they all survived. As mentioned, the friend who invited me to the party was murdered, as well as her cousin. I still don't know what exactly happened to them. I lost another close friend from Shoham who was murdered along with his partner. He got a bullet to the neck right at the beginning. The partner, who didn't want to leave him injured, called her two brothers to come to rescue them, and she was murdered along with them, so all four died. A good friend's brother was also murdered."

"What did the murders look like?" I asked.

Yonatan took a deep breath before replying, "The terrorists just went car by car, murdering everyone inside. And it wasn't just one or two bullets. There were hundreds of bullets. They sprayed people in heaps, as you can imagine, sitting ducks. Run, and you'll get shot."

"And how are you coping?" I tried to appeal to Yonatan's emotions and find out.

"I don't know. I honestly don't know. I'm still jittery; I still don't really understand where I was. The state doesn't understand where I was, either. I'm still shocked that I'm alive. I still ask myself how the person who was next to me was murdered, and I'm still alive," Yonatan said.

"Are you feeling guilt that you survived and others didn't?" I asked him, worried about the sensitivity of the question.

He did not hesitate. "Yes, I am. Even on the ones I couldn't save. On the other hand, I had no other option but to survive."

I tried to find out what the meeting with his parents, who returned to Israel the day after the attack, was like.

"My brother informed them what happened, but they didn't understand how big the chaos was. When I saw them, it was the first, last and only time I cried since October 7th. I didn't even cry at my friends' funerals. It was strange to see them. In general, I'm still trying to comprehend the whole situation. Every day feels like the attack happened yesterday. People continue with their lives, and I'm still living it."

"And what do you feel about the failure that occurred, and in general, about our future safety as a country?" It was vital for me to know because, even though he asked for help in Yonatan's case, the security forces who fell victim to the exact circumstances couldn't assist him.

"I think everything will return to normal, but not in a good way. I'm afraid we won't win, and they'll come back to kill us. I'm not optimistic about this. I'm not angry with the forces on the ground, but the truth must be told. Ultimately, they conquered us with pickup trucks, flip-flops, and bandanas on their heads. We brag about how strong our army is and our advanced technology, and in the end, we fight some people with flip-flops and losses. No matter how much we built, planned and defended, nothing helped."

Ariel Ohana

"I snorted MMC, my sister took MD, my cousin did acid. The attack started, and they wanted to stay and do drugs."

"I bought the tickets for the party that same day," Ariel Ohana, a twenty-four-year-old from Rishon Lezion, who in the past served as an IDF fighter and now manages a restaurant, told me. "I took my car to the party and drove my older cousin Eden, my cousin Roi, and my little sister Rotem. We arrived at the party at about 3:00 a.m. It was impossible to enter the party if you were under twenty-one, but we brought fake IDs with us, so we all managed to enter," she said about the beginning of the party.

Ariel shared that from the moment she and her family arrived at the party, they started using drugs.

"When we arrived at 3:00 a.m., I bumped (snorted) MMC, but it didn't affect me. At around 6:00 a.m., I smoked a joint (weed), and I was supposed to do MD (ecstasy) as well. I had the drug in a bag in my pocket, and I had already mixed it in a bottle of flavored water, but just before I drank it, the missiles started. My cousin and sister had already finished their MD, and my cousin Roi did acid (LSD)."

Ariel said that even when they started hearing the noises of the explosions, they still did not understand what it was about.

"We heard explosions. Some people started to get stressed, but because there was still music, we thought it was very high-quality effects from the speakers at the party. I realized it was a different event only after a few minutes because people started behaving strangely and stopped dancing. I saw several people who were very stressed, among them a friend of my little sister, who was anxious

194

and almost passed out. I tried to calm her down and explain that it was only rockets and that we would soon reach the Migunit and everything would be fine." At that point, I was with my sister, her friend, and my cousin. We couldn't find my cousin Roi in the party area, even though we were told that they put him in the 'safe haven,' a nickname for an organized area where people who 'got a bad trip' were taken care of. We started thinking about what to do under the pressure. I felt like I needed to throw up, probably because the joint I was smoking made my mouth dry, and I had no water available. We were scared and confused," she said.

Finally, Ariel and her family managed to find Roi, but he had a horrible trip and had trouble functioning.

"We had to put his shoes on his feet because he just looked at the sky and smiled; he wasn't able to do anything else," Ariel described the condition of her cousin Roi. It was not an unusual situation considering the fact that he had taken a powerful psychedelic drug that dramatically affects motor function and the sense of time and place and may even cause a loss of identity.

Ariel's cousin was also under the significant influence of drugs, and she wanted to stay at the party despite the alarms and missiles.

"She was very high and didn't want to leave. She was looking to do more drugs and wanted to stay with her friends. For half an hour, I found myself trying to convince my family members to get away from there. And really, only after about thirty minutes, I could drag them out of the party towards the car," Ariel said while rolling her eyes up.

"I realized that there was no use to help the injured. The terrorists would get there anyway and kill everyone."

"Afterwards, we got to my jeep, all four members of the family, and started to go up a dirt road that leads to Road 232, the central one that surrounds the Gaza border, but because a traffic jam started on that road, I could bypass everyone through the open areas with my jeep and reach the road, and that's what I did. When we arrived with the car in the Re'im area, I saw a Migunit full of people. The situation was the same at the IDF base 'Re'im Camp.' We had no place to go to, so we had to turn back," said Ariel, who, in retrospect, realized that it was probably a miracle because many of the shelters in Re'im became death traps.

After that, she returned to the same jammed dirt road she had been on. A few minutes into the traffic, a red car filled with bullet holes passed her by. All its passengers seemed to be bent over so that it was not even possible to see their faces.

"The car stopped right next to me. People got out to try to help the injured passengers who were shot, and I also brought them the tourniquet that I happened to have in the car. That was when we realized we had to run away from there. It sounds bad, but at that moment, I realized there was no use to stay and help those people who were injured because the terrorists would get there and kill everyone anyway, so there was really no one to save," she said painfully.

Ariel said that since they started to feel and even hear the sounds of gunfire getting closer and closer, they realized they had to abandon their car that was stuck in traffic and start fleeing on foot.

"Everyone started running towards the east, and so did we. We started running drunk and high. I know that in those minutes, my cousins and my sister didn't understand the situation at all, even though they heard the shots. We kept running until we reached the side of a mountain. We didn't know whether to pass it or stay there and hide. In general, the decision-making thing was terrifying. You know, if you make the wrong choice, you die."

But as the minutes passed, the sharp bursts of gunfire were heard again, and Ariel and her family members had no choice but to continue their escape.

"We had to get off the mountain. I remember that while we were running down, my cousin Roi (who took the psychedelic drug LSD) kept disappearing. He didn't understand what was happening at all. He was sure we were running away from the music; he was angry with us. He would look at us, laugh and run away as if it was a game, and all of this was happening in the midst of the inferno. He didn't cooperate at all. In my opinion, Roi was in the worst condition of anyone at the entire party. I saw people who were stoned, but I didn't see another one like him," she said.

She also said that they tried in every way to calm Roi down but with no success.

"We went down the mountain towards the fields and ran there for two hours. If we looked to the right, we saw bullets. If we looked to the left, we saw weapons aimed at us. If we ran straight, we saw weapons as well. We saw black figures in the field but couldn't recognize if they were terrorists or our security forces. The terrorists just stood on a hill and shot everyone.

In the midst of all this, in the field and during the run, we lost Roi many times, even though he could barely move. He playfully 'played tricks on us'. He was so stoned that he was looking for love, and he started hugging us tightly and didn't let go. He wouldn't agree to continue running if we didn't hug him back. We, for our part, were terribly stressed due to the firing of guns and did not know what to do or how to calm him down. We often asked for someone to help, but people were scared of him and ran away from us. At that point, everyone tried to survive on their own."

"Roi got lost. We knew the odds were not in our favor."

The incessant attempts of Ariel and her family members to keep Roi close to them succeeded only for a little while. But then, they lost him.

"Roi got lost. We couldn't find him. We kept hiding in a pit under a tree because, at that point, the shots were aimed directly in our direction. We heard the bullets whistling very loudly. We hid until the terrorists passed us, and the sound of the shots was less loud. Only then did we get out and continue our escape. During all that time, we had no idea what happened to Roi," Ariel told me.

After the girls continued their run, they found a convoy of abandoned vehicles and chose one of them to escape the party area. That arbitrary choice will become dramatic and unfathomable afterward.

"We were just the three girls, and we got into a car that had its engine on but had been abandoned for a few hours. Later on, we were joined by other runaways in the car, so seven of us were in it. We even wanted to put more in, but we didn't know how to open the trunk since the car wasn't ours, and there was no more room in the car itself. We had no phone reception either, so we didn't know how or where to navigate. It was terrifying because we knew that the terrorists were walking around the kibbutzim and on the roads in white cars. We had no idea which way we were heading and based our escape on pure luck.

Finally, the group managed to reach the main road. Ariel said that she looked out the window and saw a giant mushroom cloud from a missile hit, but it was the least of her problems because all that time, she and the girls had no idea what had happened to their cousin Roi, who was left behind in the party area.

"His mom kept calling us and asking where he was. We didn't want to answer her so as not to stress her out, and we also had no answers. We tried to contact him but with no success."

Ariel continued. "We knew that the odds were not in his favor because everyone who ran from the party would be concerned about their own survival, and Roi was not in a situation that was easy to handle. He acted scary and was so stoned that he would grab girls by the hand and beg them to run away with him. 'It's set from above, it's fate...' He would tell those girls who started to get scared and screamed and other men who saw what was happening and got mad at him."

Meanwhile, Ariel, her little sister Rotem and her cousin Eden were evacuated to Moshav Patish.

"While we were on our way there, I received a phone call from an unknown number. It was Roi who had called me from another phone after he had lost his device. The one who agreed to give him the number despite his behavior was a girl who, incomprehensibly, managed to calm him down and take care of him, something that I didn't even think was possible," she said.

That mysterious girl went as far as to accompany him all the time during their escape from the terrorists and, eventually, took him to a meeting point so he could be reunited with his family.

But the miracles didn't end there, and when the three girls were reunited with Roi in Patish, the four family members discovered that the abandoned car they used to escape the party to save themselves - belonged to the woman who saved Roi.

"So, the woman who found him, calmed him down, cared for him and took him to meet us was the car owner who saved us from that party," Ariel said excitedly. "So, basically, she saved us too," she smiled as I tried to comprehend her incredible story.

In fact, Ariel described a situation that was unimaginable but completely realistic. A situation in which if she hadn't chosen that particular car that was in that abandoned convoy, that is, if she had not taken the car that belonged to that woman, the woman herself could have used her car to get out of the inferno, and who knows what would have happened to Roi.

"Basically, I was supposed to take that woman's car so that she would have no way to travel and she would save my cousin," she said.

Indeed, miraculously, a completely random choice made by the three girls amid chaos and stress was the one that saved their cousin's life. It was a meaningless choice that became significant like no other, a visible miracle in the midst of all the horror.

"I can't think about sexuality and not think about rape. I just can't."

Ariel shared her feelings about the attack.

"It was all written from above, a higher power. I kept feeling the spirit of my grandfather, who passed away. My cousins, my sister and I are all his grandchildren. That evening, I wore his clothes but left them behind. I still haven't got them back, and I probably never will. I think we just made the right decisions, and any other choice would have led us to death. I'm glad I didn't wait for the police or IDF to save me. I feel proud that this is my story because it's the story I created for myself. I could have sat and waited, and it would have ended differently, but I chose to act."

Ariel also believed that if the attack had started minutes later and she had already taken her MD dose, the story would have been written differently.

"My family members were high and didn't want to leave, and I was the one who convinced them to go, so we left at exactly the right time. By the way, I kept running with the bottle of MD in my pocket and decided to throw it away so I wouldn't accidentally drink it out of thirst. But I'm almost certain that if I had taken the dose, I, like my family members, would have wanted to stay and sit in the party area, and everything would have ended differently. I feel pity for the person who was stoned alone, without anyone to help him because the person who took the drugs did not know what was going on around him, and he had no way to escape and save himself."

I asked Ariel about her relationship with her family members during all the infernal hours and the escape, to which she replied, "I called several people, but no one understood the situation we were in. My father went crazy; he was stressed. Actually, the worst thing happened with a friend of my sister's. She had an anxiety attack and talked to her father, who didn't stay away and came to try to rescue her. She did get out of that inferno alive, but he, who wasn't there in the first place and came to try and rescue her, was murdered."

On the other hand, Ariel shared another miracle that happened to her after I mentioned that I guess she never got to see her Jeep again.

"It's just crazy. If you look at the vehicles that were left at the party area today, you'll see that one hundred percent of them are charred, burned, and filled with bullet holes. My jeep is the only one left, white and shiny. I think the terrorists liked the white Toyota and left it alone. Ultimately, they didn't even take it. They just looted its contents."

"And how are you dealing with the situation?" I tried to find out, as Ariel seemed strong and determined.

"I had several nightmares, and at first, I was very much scared of everything. However, I will not let it affect or prevent me from doing things. Yes, it is important for me to note that in those terrible moments, I felt things I had never experienced in my life. The whole event opened up a different set of emotions for me. I appreciate and view life differently. I don't even regret that I went. Of course, if the story had ended differently, I would have said different things if I had lost someone. But under the circumstances, I appreciate the insights about life that I got from what happened."

In conclusion, it was important for me to find out if there is any message she would like to convey or any emotion close to her heart that she feels the need to share.

She nodded her head.

"Fortunately, I was not sexually assaulted at the party. And yet, as a woman, I feel the horrors that took place. Since the party, and even today - I am unable to talk to people about sexual issues. I keep imagining what happened behind me or what would have happened to me If I had decided to stay in the party area. I was afraid that someone would come and shoot me, but I didn't know that I also should have been afraid that someone would abuse me. The sexual abuse that was there does not allow me to think about sexuality without thinking about rape. That is the automatic connection that has been formed in my head ever since. Every time I hear about sexuality, I can't. I just can't. What comes to my mind is rape."

"In your opinion, is there any way that you could work on it and succeed, in the short or the long term, to not connect sexuality and sex directly to rape?" I had to inquire gently to get her honest answer.

"I'm sure it will pass, but it still surrounds me right now, and I feel so sorry and scared. To tell you the truth, I simply feel guilty, guilty for the other poor women whose lives have been ruined. As far as I'm concerned, this is the most horrible thing that happened in this war. There's dying, and there's dying, and those who were murdered after being raped died most brutally. I also talk to other girls who were at the party, and we all feel the same."

Itamar Josef

"She was shot in the head at point blank. Her brain exploded."

Itamar Josef, a twenty-six-year-old from Beit Arif, was not another raver who came to the party in Nova just to celebrate but also worked there.

"I'm a fourth-year art student, and I manage artist groups mainly in Tel Aviv and its area," Itamar told me, "I've been listening to trance music since I was little, and I started going to parties at the age of sixteen, so I know everyone, and everyone knows me. In recent years, I've started working with trance productions, and as part of that collaboration, I bring my visual artists. They make art during the event to add another layer to the festival. In the last Nova, I ran the same art complex."

The art complex that Itamar talked about is the large and well-designed dome at the festival, which can be seen in all the documentation that followed it. It was a place where the revelers were given the opportunity to enjoy a calm and comfortable environment that combined different artists from different backgrounds.

"You know, art, getting high, acid, it comes together. It works, and it catches on. The producers also saw potential in it," Itamar told me. "So, the ten artists I brought and I arrived at Nova two hours before the party started to set up the equipment and organize everything, including electricity, ultraviolet lights, chargers, and more. The event started, and we created an amazing complex that the audience absolutely loved, and many people came to paint, smoke joints and drink beer. When the event started, I also poured myself a glass and snorted cocaine for a good time.' I met friends, we danced, we laughed, and it was amazing," he shared.

But at around 6:29 a.m., the music on the small dancing floor stopped, and when Itamar scanned the area to understand why, he looked at the sky and saw an incessant barrage of missiles.

"Though I knew the festival would end because I know the meticulous procedures of those big productions, I wasn't worried. I told myself, 'Those Hamas sons of bitches just ruined our event with missiles,' but I knew that I would soon get home, and it would be over. Even around 6:45 a.m., when we started hearing gunshots, we never thought for the life of us that it was Hamas. We were sure that it was IDF activity. As far as we knew, that was the case," he said.

Itamar said that at those moments, he was with a close friend of his, who was under the influence of the psychoactive drug MD and asked him to leave the area with him as soon as possible because he had bad feelings about what was going to happen.

"I told him I wasn't going anywhere without packing all my equipment, which cost thousands of shekels. I asked him to relax, but he refused and left me. As for me, I stayed in the area of the party, sat at the bar, and smoked a cigarette," Itamar said about that famous bar, which a few minutes later became the well-documented massacre scene where dozens of people were brutally murdered while hiding inside refrigerators and chemical toilet booths, trying to hide from the terrorists with no success.

"At some point, the shots got stronger and came closer to us, but I still didn't realize that they were terrorists. I went to the main stage to consult with my friends about what to do and how to proceed from here, and they pleaded with me that the party area was the safest place since that's where all the policemen were," Itamar said. At that time, he did not know that the police officers were no longer in the party area but in the traffic routes leaving it.

While he was talking to his friends, a small head peeked out from under the stage, and someone urged them to join him in hiding.

"He said that it was something much bigger than we thought and that we should hide with him under the stage. Although we were skeptical about his words, we decided to listen to him. There were about eight of us on the stage. Some watched through the sheet that wrapped it to see what was happening outside, and I was one of them," said Itamar, who says that at those exact moments, the terrorists had already entered the party area.

"The terrorists entered Nova through the second stage entrance, which was next to the restrooms and the bar where I smoked a cigarette a moment before. They murdered everyone who was there. There was a complete massacre inside the restrooms and inside the bar itself; they shot at everyone non-stop. Meanwhile, we continued to hide under the main stage while the terrorists were murdering everyone in Nova. I peeked under the stage, and I saw the terrorists murdering and kidnapping. People just ran, got shot and fell to the ground," said Itamar, who added that crazy enough, that was not the only thing he had to deal with. "At some point, I saw a huge scorpion walking right next to me, under the stage. I warned everyone, took off my shoe, crushed it and put it back on my foot."

Itamar shared more horrors that he witnessed while hiding under the stage and peeking at what was happening.

"I saw a girl who was shot in the head from point-blank range, and her brain exploded. Her whole head just exploded. I saw two other girls who were simply executed. They didn't mess with them at all. They just shot them once in the head and blew it up."

Itamar said that although he saw the people being murdered before his eyes, at those moments, he still did not understand the magnitude of what was happening.

"Suddenly, someone lifted the sheet that was around the stage and exposed us. He shouted that we had to get out of there and run and that we were awaiting our death like sheep to the slaughter. At that moment, I decided to listen to him, left the stage, and started running, followed by a large group of other people who did the same as me. What we did not know was that the terrorists saw us.

They started shooting at us non-stop. People fell after getting hit. I managed to dodge, run, and reach an open potato field. An area that was already full of bodies. At one point, while the terrorists were shooting at me, I came across two women who were lying wounded on the ground, and I stopped to check their pulses, but they were dead bodies," Itamar said, and after I asked for specifics he added, "one of them was shot with two bullets in the buttock, and the other was lying on the ground in a position that made no sense. She didn't look like a normal person."

For a long while, Itamar and his friends who escaped with him hid in hiding places, kept running and dodged the terrorists' shots intermittently.

"In the hiding places, the shots were so close that the dirt from the bullet smashing into the ground flew into our faces. The bullets passed by our heads. They aimed especially at us," he said. "At a certain point, we arrived at a seasonal creek that had no water at all, completely dry, and on its other bank, we saw ten Arabs coming our way. We didn't know if they were terrorists or Israeli citizens who didn't want to harm us. My friend who was next to me claimed that we should wait for them and that they would tell us what was going on, and I told him that they looked like terrorists to me and that we should run away."

Eventually, Itamar and his friends decided to wait for those guys.

Unfortunately, Itamar's gut feeling was not far from the truth.

"They came to us and grabbed my friend's bag, and one of them started beating him on the head with a stick. That friend punched the guy who grabbed him, and together, we started running toward that dry creek. We ran for our lives. Those guys, who were Gaza citizens, entered through breaches in the fence and apparently came to rob us or kidnap us. They followed us but didn't even run. Luckily, they had no weapons," he said.

At one point during the run, Itamar and his friends spotted a large tree with Israelis hiding under it and decided to join them.

"The Gazans saw that we had joined a larger group and decided not to advance. We stayed in the same hiding place for about two hours and continued to hear bullets whistling from everywhere and from every angle, above us and in our direction, by terrorists passing through the area. During this time, we tried to make countless calls to the IDF, the police, the MDA, the officers we knew from the army, and the commanders of our units from the past. We were hoping that someone would come to rescue us, but no one was able to get close to us at all, and there was no one to reach us. There were even IDF helicopters that passed over us, lowered their altitude and shone on us to examine who we were, but they didn't land for us because they simply couldn't face the terrorists' anti-tank missiles," Itamar shared the apocalyptic and painful situation in which the Israel Defense Forces was unable to help its citizens in need of rescue, even though the soldiers were aware of their whereabouts.

"Did you get the chance to call your family?" I asked Itamar, who painfully replied, "My mom passed away two years ago, so I called my father from another phone because my battery had long since run out. He decided to set out to come and rescue me, but I told him to stay away loud and clear because I knew they would kill him."

Meanwhile, those Gaza citizens who had decided to avoid confrontation earlier returned again, this time in double numbers. They urged Itamar and his friends to come out of hiding. With unimaginable resourcefulness, that group of hideouts decided to fight back.

"We were assertive. We started picking up planks and stones and got prepared to kick their asses. We realized that we were fighting for our lives. We started arming ourselves with everything that came by and ran to them," he said.

Indeed, Itamar and his friends from the hiding place boldly came out of it, with stones and boards in their hands, and ran towards the Gaza citizens while a barrage of bullets was fired at them by terrorists who were constantly in the area.

"There were so many bullets fired at us that you couldn't even tell from which direction they came. Nevertheless, we continued to run with all our strength towards the Gazans and fought them. Those Gazans saw that we were prepared for a real battle, got scared and ran away," Itamar said.

"He shot an RPG missile at us. People flew through the air, one guy was completely blown up, and his organs were thrown everywhere. I too got hit very hard in the head."

Not much time passed from the moment Itamar and his friends succeeded, with great courage, in chasing away the Gaza citizens before they had to face another threat. A threat that was much more menacing and, unfortunately, ended in a fatal way.

"I saw a guy standing about three hundred feet from us and didn't stop staring at us and checking us out. He was dressed all in black and had a huge black bag on his back. I was very stressed by the bag. At that point, I saw a lot of terrorists around me, but I hadn't seen a terrorist with a huge bag like that on his back. I began to tell all my friends in the hiding place, which had about forty people, that a suspicious man was looking at us with a bag. The minutes passed, and we kept staring at the person who did not move and only stared back at us," Itamar said dramatically, justly so.

Itamar further said that the same guy in black was standing alone, and suddenly, out of the trees he was standing next to, a mysterious girl emerged. That girl stood next to him for a few seconds until she directly and unhesitatingly pointed clearly and unmistakably at Itamar and his group of friends.

Of course, Itamar was filled with suspicion, but he also did not expect what was to come.

"She just pointed at us in a direct line. At that moment, I got up from my lying position and drew everyone's attention because that girl was weirdly pointing at us. I told them that something was not right. At those moments, the guy got down on his knees in a kneeling position. As we saw that, everybody started to scatter and run in all directions," Itamar said. "Not a second passed, and he released an RPG missile at us. The missile exploded in the middle of the circle that we formed while we ran, but with a slight angle, and at least four people went flying into the air. I got hit by the shock wave and got thrown almost four feet from where I stood. I hit my head very hard. Thinking about it, I probably also had a concussion because I was really dizzy. We just kept running, each in a different direction without looking at others, and we split up. I kept running and was left alone while the terrorist and his friends, who had joined him, continued to shoot us with a Kalashnikov without stopping. They aimed and fired. They didn't care who they hit – the more, the better. I started running in zigzags, and the bullets passed by my head; I heard them so loudly. It was a miracle they didn't hit me at that time." Itamar told me about that horrendous moment.

He also mentioned that if he hadn't noticed that guy dressed in black, all those forty people would have been killed on the spot.

"If I hadn't looked at him again and again and decided that he seemed suspicious to me, then nobody would have cared, and the results would have been different. Just because I did not like his stare, I urged everyone to be alert and pay attention. Luckily, he hit the ground at an angle because otherwise, he would have hit us directly and would have killed more, and a mass of people would have exploded."

I asked Itamar to describe what the explosion looked like.

"I saw four people flying through the air. There was one guy who was completely blown up. Apparently, the missile hit him directly and blew up his entire body. Of course, I didn't stay behind to pick up his body parts. I kept running. But I definitely saw things flying in the air. I can't tell you if it was a head, a piece of brain or a hand, but you saw organs just flying in the air. I have also seen people fly six or seven feet in the air from the shock wave, others got hit severely from shrapnel, and there were those who survived and were kidnapped afterward," Itamar, who was injured as well, said.

He got up from his chair and showed me his phone. It got lost in the explosion and was later found. That device was utterly broken and smashed, and of course, today, Itamar is using a new one. His glasses also did not survive the shock wave. They fell and shattered completely. He continued his escape with one shattered part of one lens to try to see the area and survive.

I tried to find out more about the identity of that mysterious girl.

"I have no idea who she was, and no one knows. Maybe she was a Gazan, and there is even a chance that she was an Israeli girl who got kidnapped and was threatened at gunpoint. Maybe they told her that if she pointed out the hiding place of a group of Israelis, they would release her. But there is no way to know for sure," Itamar said.

"I found myself squeezed between two bodies in a ditch. I couldn't move."

Itamar describes the area he fled to after the missile hit as a small forest full of trees, among which he ran and hid.

"I crouched down behind one of the trees whose trunk was large. At least four bullets aimed at me hit the tree. I stayed there for a few minutes when, at this point, I was completely alone, and all my friends had already separated from me due to the impact of the RPG. I peeked through a crack in the trunk of the tree, and I saw terrorists shooting at the ground. I wasn't very interested in what they were doing. I guess they were confirming the killings. As soon as I saw that they were busy, I took the opportunity and ran back to a potato field."

According to Itamar, the plantation was well plowed, a large agricultural area with deep ditches that made it difficult to walk normally. You could only navigate it by carefully skipping between the holes.

"I jumped backward to the first trench that was there and got into it. I raised my head to take a look and see what was happening outside, and one of the terrorists caught my movement. He shot directly into that trench, and when I caught it, I immediately lowered my head. And in a matter of a millisecond, the bullet passed by me and hit the back side of the trench I was lying in. After that, he fired two more bullets, which hit the same spot, and one of the hot bullets bounced from the ground to my shoulder." Itamar continued, "The bullet was scorching hot and caused a burn in my shoulder. I tried to move my arm and get it off me, but I only managed to roll it to the back of my neck. Despite the unbearable pain, I couldn't get out, and I had to deal with the injury inside the trench itself. As mentioned, the terrorist knew I was there, and I was one hundred percent sure that he would come over to make sure I was dead, so, in my head, I started to make a speech in English and thought about what I was going to tell him so that he wouldn't kill me. I thought to tell him that I had money, that I was an important man in Israel, and that he should kidnap me and not kill me. I also planned ahead that if I saw him cocking the weapon and coming to kill me, then I'll jump on him, try to take some rocks and bash his head. I decided that if I were going to die, I'd die while fighting."

Miraculously, something that didn't happen very much on October 7th occurred. The terrorist was apparently busy with other things and did not check Itamar.

"Using the scratched lens that I still had in my hand, I lifted my head above the ditch once more and peeked out. There was an insane number of terrorists there, dozens. But I saw that they were busy with different things, and I took the opportunity to jump into another ditch."

And so, each time, Itamar waited in inspiring patience for the right moment, jumped another ditch, and kept doing that for about twenty holes.

"On the way, of course, I came across bodies that were in the trenches - a body above or below me. During one of the jumps, I saw out of the corner of my eye a hand sticking out of one of the trenches a few feet from me just a hand. That's it. Although I focused on my own survival, at some point in one of the trenches I reached, I couldn't take it anymore.

It was about 1:30 p.m., and I hadn't had any water for at least six hours. I was thirsty and dehydrated, and because I had also done some cocaine at the party, my mouth was dry. Even while hiding, I smoked cigarettes, so I really started to feel like I was dehydrating;

this is in addition to the blow I received in my head from the RPG. The bullet burns still hurt, as well as the bruises that covered my body from the continuous running and hiding. My whole body was bruised on an appalling level. All over were scratches and cuts. I was bleeding. With all this, I had to find a solution."

Itamar said that he decided to take a risk and jump three ditches at once because he had to find a water source.

"So, I jumped into the ditch and felt like I hit my head on a rock. When I tried to move that rock, it didn't budge. I studied the ditch a bit better and then saw that the 'rock' was actually some guy's shoe. I looked again and saw that the guy was already dead. I immediately shuffled backward, which was really difficult since I was lying in a fetal position in the ditch. As I moved, my feet slammed into another 'rock.' When I tried to move this rock this time, I saw that it was the head of a redheaded woman. She was also dead. In fact, right in the ditch I entered, there were two bodies of a man and a woman, which, at first glance, I didn't see at all," he shared painfully.

In those moments, Itamar's ordeal was terrible, to say the least. But he had no choice but to remain stuck and squeeze between the two bodies next to him in a small but deep ditch, in a situation that reminded me, once again, of the death pits in the Holocaust. Itamar recited the 'Shema Israel[3]' prayer and spoke in his heart to his mother, who passed away about two years ago. 'Mom, look where I am. Please, save me,' he begged as he was getting more and more dehydrated without an available source of water.

"At one point, I saw a pipe near the ditch and reached for it, hoping there would be water in it. I pulled the pipe towards me and

_____

3. The central affirmation of Judaism. The prayer expresses belief in the singularity of God, that is, in God's oneness and incomparability.

flipped over. My head was so close to the dead red-haired girl's head, and in fact, my feet had touched hers all the time. I checked the pipe, but there was no water in it. I broke it completely just to make sure, but nothing, it was empty," Itamar shared his horrors.

He jumped into a different ditch to get away from the two bodies that were next to him, and there he realized that if he didn't get ready access to fluids, he would have no way to survive.

"I told myself I wasn't going to die. On the other hand, I didn't have a source of water. I pushed my finger into my mouth to vomit. I didn't vomit, but thanks to the gag reflex, I was able to produce some saliva in my mouth. I spread the saliva inside my mouth to moisten it with my finger. As I had planned, I managed to swallow some saliva. I had no other choice; my throat was parched to the point that I swallowed air with complete suffocation. That's why I moistened my mouth with the saliva, and it did work," Itamar said while hiccupping during the last sentence and refusing my request to pause the interview so he could go and have a drink of water.

"There was a pregnant woman there who was just slaughtered. They cut her in every limb of her body. She was completely crushed and covered in blood."

Despite the success in obtaining a source of liquids, if it can even be defined that way, Itamar had to continue his escape.

He glanced through his broken lens one more time and saw an IDF tank and an Israeli armored police vehicle a few yards away from him.

"Next to the vehicles, I also saw survivors and a policewoman standing with a drawn weapon. I started waving at them, calling for help. The survivors who noticed me started to scream that I had to run towards them. At that moment, I got up and started running like a psychopath. I ran like crazy and also raised my hands to make it clear that I am an Israeli," Itamar said.

But the IDF soldiers were engrossed in the war and did not know who the figure that ran towards them was, so they fired a warning shot at Itamar.

Itamar stopped for a few seconds and signaled at himself in the hopes that they would recognize him and figure out that he was "one of their own."

He did not respond appropriately to the warning shot and continued running towards the vehicles. For him, it was literally a matter of life or death.

As he got closer and closer to the vehicles, some of the survivors managed to identify him and pleaded with the policewoman that he was an Israeli citizen. The policewoman did not listen to them.

"I was thirty feet away from the policewoman and the vehicles when she aimed her weapon directly at me. The IDF soldiers were lying on the ground and aimed their weapons at me as well. She asked me what my name was and completely stripped me, and then also told me to turn around. When she realized that I was one of the survivors, she agreed that I would join them, and along with about fifty survivors, soldiers, and policemen - I hid behind the tank along with them," Itamar testifies about what happened to him.

His friends who were there brought him water, hugged him, and supported him while hiding behind the tank that the soldiers who were in it were burned alive by an RPG hit earlier.

Itamar begged his friends to take him away, to get him out of the hell he had fallen into, and that he did not want to stay in the area one more minute.

Indeed, he was part of one of the initial convoys that the IDF escorted out of the area once they confirmed its location. These convoys made up of armored vehicles, led survivors, whether in their own vehicles or those provided, away from the chaos.

But think again if you thought that Itamar's story ended here, as I hoped during the interview with him.

"I boarded one of the abandoned vehicles along with my friend and two other people. We started traveling in a convoy led by an IDF police vehicle, but strangely, the armored vehicle at the front of the convoy suddenly disappeared. At that stage, we did not know where to go or where to head. We had the options of turning left towards Ofakim, continuing straight towards Re'im, or, of course, returning to the tank area. We knew that this was a fateful decision because we were in a war zone, without weapons, and we had already seen dead bodies everywhere during the drive, including two police officers in a car. I asked my friend who was driving the car to go back, but he didn't listen to me and kept driving straight. That was when we found ourselves, without any protection, in Kibbutz Ra'im," he said.

It is important to note that by the time Itamar and his car companions entered Kibbutz Re'im it was already completely taken over by Hamas's terrorists.

No one prepared Itamar for the sights that were waiting for him there.

"These were the most difficult visual sights I've ever seen: headless people and children who were shot in the streets. We saw a child just lying on the grass shot with two bullets that hit them. At the entrance to the kibbutz, we saw a pregnant girl who had just been slaughtered. They completely slaughtered her, decapitated her, and dismembered her. I don't know how. It looked like someone took two machetes and did those things to her..." Itamar waved his hand in the air in a cutting motion.

I asked him where on the pregnant woman's body were the cuts, to which he replied, "All over her body. Her whole body was completely cut."

Still, I insisted on hearing from him more specific details about the condition of that pregnant woman's body. "I saw a huge belly, and the woman had been shot and cut in every part of her body everywhere. The cuts were all over her body, including her stomach, of course. She was completely crushed. She was covered in blood," Itamar said, adding, "There were people there that were laying on the ground, dead. But they didn't have hands. They had a body, no hands. I don't know; maybe they were murdered after having their hands cut off with an ax while they screamed in pain, lost blood, and died, or they just died from the headshots. They abused all the corpses there."

I asked Itamar to share with me also the sights of the dead children.

"It's something that's terrible, that's shocking. I saw a little blond boy on the ground shot. Even in the most terrible horror movies, these things are censored. I tell everyone they are not human beings; they are not even animals; they are Satan himself, pure demons."

"The terrorists cut off people's heads and kicked them to the middle of the road. The whole road was full of heads."

Immediately after Itamar was exposed to the horrors, he ordered his friend to return to the tank. At that exact moment, the terrorists fired a bullet at their vehicle, but they managed to escape back and waited for the next convoy to arrive and take them out of the war zone.

"The road to Ofakim was shocking. Piles of corpses that were simply soaked with gasoline and set on fire. Completely burnt vehicles. Everything was filled with smoke. A lot of terrorist vehicles that were at the end of the road with their doors open were still there. A road of horrors. At some point, I asked my friend why he was driving in zigzags, and he yelled at me, 'Lift your head, you son of a bitch'. I lifted my head and couldn't believe what I was seeing. Have you seen the movie 'The Purge'? Imagine it like that, except everyone was already dead all around. Everyone," Itamar described. He was not the first survivor to choose this movie to explain the situation.

But even in the movie 'The Purge,' they did not show what Itamar witnessed on the roads of horrors. "The whole road was full of heads. Every single yard we drove was full of heads. You could see a body inside the car, but the head was outside. They placed their heads in the middle of the road just like that. People didn't want to run the head over, so they drove around it in a zigzag pattern," Itamar said and continued the harsh descriptions, "I saw a car, and the body was lying next to the car. The head of that body - just laid on the road. It looks as if the terrorists cut the head off and kicked it. This is probably what happened. After all, there is no other reason why the head is in the middle of the road and not attached to the body."

When Itamar talked about the terrorists kicking the heads into the middle of the road, all I had left to imagine with horrifying cynicism was a soccer game, with the heads actually representing the kicked ball. In those moments, I also realized how much all the testimonies I've heard and the sights I witnessed continuously changed my mind about reality and how I see and imagine things.

I understood and comprehended that writing the book would also affect me personally - and significantly.

"We snorted lines of cocaine next to the policemen inside the police car."

In Ofakim, Itamar waited for a few hours, during which he met some of his friends who survived, some of whom were wounded. From there, Itamar was taken to Kibbutz Gilat, where his father arrived with his younger brother to pick him up.

When I asked Itamar how his family received him, he said, "Until a week later, no one really understood the magnitude of what happened at the party. At first, everyone was busy with the communities and did not know about the massacre in Nova. So, when my father arrived, my little brother was anxious, and my father smiled. It was a very comforting moment to see them. Only then did I believe that I was going home. Up until then, everything was filled with question marks. But yes, they were unaware of what really happened there, and only when I told my father what I had been through - he was shocked and couldn't even believe what I experienced. We all had dinner together. I smoked a full pack of cigarettes to relax, and I also had a joint. Only then did I fall asleep like a baby. The truth is that on the first night, I didn't sleep in my room but with my father in his bed. It felt extraordinary to sleep alone, so I preferred to sleep next to someone."

"I was just going to ask - how are you dealing with the situation?" I asked Itamar, who replied, "At first, I had anxiety. For a month, I hardly left the house. However, I think I have a certain resilience. I think of the difficult images as another image from a horror movie. I treat myself to psychologists. Still, there are dreams, Yes. And does the body sometimes collapse? Yes. And are there seizures? Yes. This is the result of post-trauma. I work on myself; it's not easy, but there is no choice. I took it upon myself from this attack to continue living, and I've even been to several parties since then. Sometimes, of course, there are falls. Like, a few days ago when I was sitting with a friend and we were smoking hash - I had a post-traumatic attack - my body collapsed."

I asked him if his close friends were killed in the attack. Unfortunately, Itamar said yes.

"I lost twelve friends in the attack, and I also have two friends who were kidnapped. Of the twelve friends I lost, five were my closest friends - two of them brothers and sisters. The five of them were more like siblings, and they were murdered there. By the way, if I'm counting all of my acquaintances from the party - more than seventy were murdered. So yes, I know most of the faces that were murdered in Nova. I think it's something that the human mind comprehends in small parts. It happened to me about two weeks ago. I was at an event hosted by a friend, and the event was relatively boring. So, I said to myself, 'Come on, call Gilly' (an alias). She is a good friend of mine, and she is in love with nightlife, she will come, and we will have fun together. I took the phone out of my pocket to call her, and then I remembered that she was murdered. A bizarre situation - I put the phone back in my pocket."

A bright spot was when Itamar told me that the friend he spoke about at the beginning of the testimony, who was under the influence of the drug MD and who, at the start of the attack, left him due to his anxieties, survived.

"While he left me, the terrorists had already arrived at the party's area and started shooting people. He ran into them - and managed to escape," he said.

The story of Itamar's escape is different from that of most of the survivors since, for most of the attack, Itamar stayed in the party area itself and next to it and saw the horrors with his own eyes. I tried to find out with him how he felt about it.

"The story is really more complex. All around me, I kept seeing corpses. Suddenly, someone ran towards me with half of her face blown off by a grenade. Because of the adrenaline, she didn't even feel that half of her lip was non-existent, totally ripped off," Itamar demonstrated with his hands the way her face looked.

He shared with me how crazy the situation was, not to say apocalyptic.

"The hours of the attack were hours when you could do whatever you wanted. Even if I took girls and raped them or took a gun and killed people - no one would know it was me. It was madness. There was complete chaos. At one of the safe points on the way out of the inferno, we did bamps (snorts) of coke to relax inside a police car that picked us up. The cop ignored it, and we snorted lines of cocaine in front of him in the car. In general, the police cars picked up a lot of revelers from the party, and those revelers were high on acid (LSD), did ecstasy, and needed something to reset them. So, they started snorting lines of cocaine in the back seat of the car. It was like that for us, too. My friends started doing cocaine vamps and asked me if I wanted to. So, I looked at the policeman, and the policeman looked back at me - and pretended to be driving. I told my friends, 'Yeah, give me some,' and started snorting. Do you understand the level of chaos? The policeman didn't care at all. What mattered to him was that we were alive. The truth is, when I think about it now, we got out of a fucking massacre - so they should be grateful we didn't light some bongs in the car. And like I said, the police didn't care. What was important to them was to rescue as many people as possible and save as many people as possible."

As a former fighter, Itamar shared his opinion on the events.

"I think that this was the biggest military failure that the State of Israel had. I think that it should be judged at the highest level. I think that the senior officials in the IDF who were in charge of the army at those moments should not only resign but also sit in prison for many months. The observers alerted everyone about the attack, but the senior officials did not give a fuck, and lo and behold, it blew up in our faces. Personally, I think there was something to do with the betrayal and intelligence that the enemy received from the inside. Just think - who organized all of this? A reckless organization that the Israel Defense Forces were unable to take control of for five or six days. They surprised us - and eliminated us."

I asked Itamar if there was any important message for him to convey, to which he said, "It didn't just happen. There is a reason why God united the people of Israel now. It's all connected to each other. 'Am Israel chai, the people of Israel are still alive, and they will exist, and they will always exist - no matter how many times they try to destroy us. We will always stay here. What I personally took upon myself from this attack is to continue living. God gave me a chance to live once again, and I will live, and I will absorb this life into me, and I will relish them – all this while being Jewish all the time, and I will endow my Jewish roots to everyone. I believe in the Jew in me, and I believe in Judaism."

Guy Ben Shimon

"Her buttocks and thighs were riddled with bullets. She was conscious and screaming in pain."

I met Guy Ben Shimon, a twenty-four-year-old from Oranit, while he was playing the guitar.

Guy is a musician as well as a martial arts athlete. He bought the ticket for the Nova festival about two hours before it opened, following a spontaneous suggestion from his friend Daria to come with her to the party.

"We arrived at about 2:00 a.m., me, Daria, a close friend and two other girlfriends. The party was exceptional, and I had the opportunity to talk with people I hadn't seen in a long time. At about 6:30 a.m., the missiles started; there were many missiles. At first, I didn't understand at all that those were rockets. I was sure it was the music. After being warned that it was a 'Red Alert,' we started walking towards the vehicles. My friends and I had to split up since they live elsewhere in the country, and I was already planning to go home alone without them in a different car," said Guy about the beginning of the attack. At that moment, he thought it was just a missile attack.

Guy started his journey, apparently, to the center of the country, but on his way along Road 232, he started getting warning signs about what was happening at the end of the road.

"Cars came back in the opposite direction. People were waving and yelling at us from the windows not to continue driving straight but to turn around because there were shots and a pickup truck full of terrorists on the way. I was skeptical, but there was a guy who stopped me and just showed me a video he had taken a few minutes before. The video showed armed men in uniform in a white pickup. They were shooting at his car. I didn't take a risk and turned around. I stopped my car and thought about what to do while an IDF officer arrived in the area and directed everyone to the east. At that point, a group of about a thousand people started running east, but I wasn't one of them. I was curious and decided to stay on the road," he said.

And so, in a questionable decision, Guy remained on the road even though most of the revelers fled to the east.

"Every few minutes, we heard the whistling of bullets coming closer. At one point, I heard deafening screams from a girl. I went towards the noise to find out what was going on, and then I saw her. Her whole buttock was riddled with bullets, and her thighs as well. The whole lower area was just perforated. At those moments, some guys brought a stretcher, which, in hindsight, I knew was there for the party. They undressed the girl and started putting a tourniquet on her," Guy shared the dramatic moments and the difficult sights.

He said that despite the severe injuries, the girl was still conscious and, therefore, did not stop screaming in pain.

"While she continued to scream, and the whistles of the bullets were only getting closer to us, me and three other guys lifted her onto the stretcher and ran with her towards the ambulance, which was also there for the party. While we were running with her, the wounded girl went limp on the stretcher and many times almost fell; this was due to the sharp turns we had to do during the run that was forced on us to escape from the terrorists and to get her treated as quickly as possible," Guy said, "and in the process, she screamed in pain, horrible screams."

"The policeman gave me a loaded gun and urged me to shoot the terrorists."

When Guy and the guys that were with him managed to get that girl into the ambulance, the terrorists were already right next to them. Guy said that each of them took a different cover to hide.

"I jumped to the right side of the road and hid behind everything I could, and then the bullets started coming. The bullets whistled from all sides, and I heard screams non-stop. At one point, I moved my head, and a bullet just flew over my brain and hit the leaf above my head," he described while demonstrating the situation.

Guy shared that during those moments of terror, he was also in contact with his mother on his phone, and at my request, he talked about the content of that conversation.

"The gunshot whistled next to me, and the bullets flew over my head. First, I sent her a video of the bullet that passed over my head and hit the leaf, and then I talked to her on the phone and told her that I was being shot at and that I loved her. My mom reacted like a lioness. She begged me to be quiet, to hang up the phone, and to call her after I found a place to hide. In retrospect, I know she was broken but also unusually cool and composed," Guy said. "The terrorists were about seventy feet from me. I counted to three and decided that I was running towards the east so as not to be killed as a sheep to the slaughter. While I was running for my life, the terrorists launched an RPG missile at an Apache helicopter. I saw the missile passing near the helicopter's tail but did not hit it. About ten people were running madly through rice paddies with bullets flying in the air. After hours without water or food, we found ourselves in a bell pepper field where we hid and ate the peppers," he said.

Guy continued the escape in the area together with two more people who were also running for their lives, and he did not expect what would happen next.

"Suddenly, after a few more miles of running, we noticed a black jeep driven by a policeman in uniform in the middle of the field. We didn't know whether to trust it or not because, at this stage, we already understood that some of the terrorists had enough time to wear Israeli IDF or police uniforms. We decided to take the risk and got into the car. I sat in the passenger seat, and the two people that were with me sat in the back. In one moment, the policeman pulled out a gun. He gave it to me, announced that the gun was loaded, opened the window, and drove at a crazy speed. He urged me that if I saw a terrorist on the way, just to shoot him," Guy said.

That policeman was busy driving so fast in an area that was not designed for moving vehicles that he decided to give his weapon to Guy, who was a completely random citizen so that he could manage the situation for him.

"There was a terrorist squad behind us, and the policeman had to have both hands on the wheel so that the car wouldn't overturn in the field, so he just decided to put his trust in me. In general, he seemed completely shocked. Suddenly, that policeman gets a phone call and starts speaking in Arabic. The guys behind me and I didn't know what to do. We were worried that maybe he was a terrorist who decided to kidnap us to Gaza and give us the gun to gain our trust. We got stressed and had to take action. The friend behind me placed both hands on the front seat next to the driver's neck as if he were ready to grab him if necessary. I yelled at him to tell me his name and to stop the car immediately," Guy said about the confusing situation.

The driver stopped his vehicle at Guy's request, and the three abandoned the car and continued to move on foot.

They never had the chance to thank him because they weren't sure of who he was, but in hindsight, Guy realized that it was indeed an Israeli policeman, an Arabic-speaking Druze, who risked his life trying to save him and his escape partners.

We can only wonder how apocalyptic the situation was.

Young Israelis who were in danger and ran for their lives had no way of knowing if they had found a place of safety with a policeman who came to their rescue or if they were being kidnapped to the Gaza Strip by a mastermind terrorist.

And what about the policeman's decision to give his weapon to a random person he didn't know at all, who had no license or training to possess or use a gun because he simply had no other choice? Indeed, these situations, somewhat delusional, were experienced by the victims and survivors of the October 7th massacre.

"Friends were murdered. Girlfriends were kidnapped and shot."

Guy and his friends continued to flee on foot for about three miles until they reached a greenhouse compound that was run by Thai workers, where they found an Israeli guy who would take them in his car to a gas station at the Urim intersection. In that station, someone received a heads-up that a terrorist was getting closer to the area with an RPG lunger in his hand. Meanwhile, Guy continued to witness the horrors, even at the gas station, and noticed two Israelis whose ribs were open because they were shot multiple times. He proceeded to run to the Moshav Patish area, where he also faced massive rocket fire at him, and then found his way back home.

I asked him what happened to the wounded woman, the one that he tried to rescue after she was shot in the lower part of her body.

His answer was shocking.

"That girl died from her wounds. On top of that, two of the guys who helped me lift the stretcher and treated her medically were also murdered. Only I and one other survived that situation."

"You told me that you came to the party with five friends and that you had to split up from them at the beginning of the escape journey. What happened to them?" I asked Guy, who took a deep breath and detailed his four friends' different endings.

"Daria, the friend who invited me to the party in the first place, survived. On the other hand, my friend who was with us was murdered that day. The third friend (a girl) was kidnapped to Gaza and later was murdered in captivity by Hamas, and the other friend got shot three times and survived."

In my creative but unbearably painful thoughts, I imagined Guy's story as the children's book "The Story of Five Balloons[4]," only this time it was the story of five young kids, young people, and here, too, each of them had a different end. While Guy and Daria survived, their third friend was murdered in an attack, another friend was kidnapped to the Gaza Strip and murdered in captivity, and the fifth was seriously injured. The worst thing of all is, of course, that this is not a children's story, and unfortunately, not a story at all but a painful and cruel reality of a group of friends that fell apart.

But Guy's pain and loss did not end there.

"Ron (an alias) was a close friend with whom I worked at the beach for a year. A week before the party, we arranged to meet, but in the end, it didn't work out. He was murdered at the party," he said.

With resounding insensitivity, I would say even cruelly, though consciously, I asked Guy if he was the one who canceled the meeting with his close friend who had been murdered.

Guy put a half smile on his face, indicating great embarrassment, and said, "Yes, I canceled it."

I apologized, but nevertheless, I asked if he felt guilty, and Guy said no.

"I don't feel guilty, but I do have a feeling of missing out. Maybe I could have given him a good, big hug."

"And how are you coping so far?" I asked Guy.

He replied, "I feel like I'm getting stronger. It's a process that involves a lot of pain based on meeting this evil and seeing that there is such evil in the world. It's indescribable."

---

4. A classic Israeli children's book.

In an attempt to refute the accusations in the international community against the activities of Israel in general and the IDF in particular in the Gaza Strip, Guy added, "Even Buddha would slap someone sometimes. That is, even the most peace-loving person will sometimes give a slap. There is a time for peace; we'll choose that option most of the time. But there is also a time for war, and in war, people will be killed, unfortunately also innocent people. Hamas crossed a line that cannot be crossed ethically, humane and morally."

Chapter Four

It's Enough To Be Human

In the last few months, I have been interviewing, documenting, listening, summarizing, absorbing, and, above all, getting immersed in thoughts about the dozens of unimaginable testimonies of the events of October 7th and after. I'll admit, my nights are no longer the same quiet nights, my soul is no longer as innocent as it was, and the agony is nothing less than cruel. As a third-generation Holocaust survivor, while listening to the unbearably difficult sequence of testimonies, I understand that if it were possible to photograph the Holocaust of the Jewish people in World War II, the scenes would be similar to those that took place on October 7th.

It occurred to me that while the survivors of the Nazi Holocaust are dwindling, the nation of Israel is adding to its lot a new generation of survivors—the survivors of October 2023.

Although the comparison to the extermination of six million Jews is unbearably difficult and may even provoke criticism, I insist that the sights I was exposed to and the evidence I described in this book do constitute proof of the existence of pure, systematic, planned and horrifyingly meticulous evil. Evil, which human history will discuss for hundreds of years to come, and even then, I doubt that anyone will be able to find a satisfactory explanation of how a person becomes a devil, thus performing actions that a human mind cannot understand or comprehend.

To make sure that there will not be a person in the world who can deny or challenge the very existence of the massacre, the atrocities and the terror, I worked on building an eternal, authentic and chilling set of evidence, the assembly of which was not easy at all.

During my many meetings, I had to dive into the depths of the victims' wounded souls and raise unbearably difficult and some-times insensitive questions. I had to insist on the exact, specific, and cruel details of the horrors that they experienced and saw with their own eyes only a concise while ago. These retellings may have "returned" them to the moments of inferno and horror and recre-ated the pain, fear, grief, and loss they are still trying to overcome, sometimes with no success.

I did all this out of a sense of obligation and duty and with a primary, higher, significant goal like no other, such that its impor-tance cannot be disputed. This mission is to immortalize for eter-nity the murder, the rape, the abuse, the torture, the burning, the cutting, the dismemberment, the suffocation, the strangulation and the disfiguration of the bodies that were carried out on babies, toddlers, children, pregnant women, men, the elderly and soldiers by the damned Hamas terrorists, by the operatives of the terrorist organizations and by everyone who participated no matter how big or small in a massacre unprecedented in its cruelty, for which there is no forgiveness.

The commemoration, memory and preservation of the historical events in this book are not only expressed by being painful, sharp, shocking and horrendous, but first and foremost, their purpose is to convey an unambiguous message:

It is not at all necessary to be an Israeli citizen to be pained by the atrocities and the massacre that were committed and to wonder what is such a dark and unfathomable evil that turns quiet kibbutzim into extermination camps or a rave party into a bloodbath, one that slaughters those who just wanted to dance, one that abuses entire families.

It is not at all necessary to be a member of the Jewish religion to sympathize with the last heartbeats of a mother who watches her little children burn before her eyes and cannot do anything, or with the bursting and helpless cries of a toddler whose father's protective and caring hands are cruelly dropped from him.

It is not at all necessary to be a woman to be enraged to the depths of our souls by the suffering of that girl who was tied to a tree and brutally raped many times or the one who was sexually assaulted after having metal wires inserted into her body.

It is not at all necessary to be a parent to cry and feel bitter about the horribly innocent eyes of a small child who doesn't understand why people, seemingly just like him, hurt him and torture him to the point of bleeding and then cut off his limbs or slit his throat even though he did nothing to them, or the universe in general. His only sin was that he wanted to laugh, smile, play and dream.

It is not necessary to be a scholar to understand that the revenge of October 7th, 2023, has not yet been created, even by Satan himself.

It's enough to be human.

Chapter Five

The Statement of Israel's State President, Mr. Isaac Herzog

A hundred days have passed since life stopped, the sky darkened, and we, all of us, were exposed to a boiling and shocking lava of pure hatred that was poured over us.

A hundred days of an indeed just war and a test for the entire nation. It is a test of courage, bravery, determination, righteousness, strength, solidarity, unity, and our commitment as a society to the values and principles that define us as a nation.

In these difficult times, we cannot help but reflect on the sacrifice of our daughters and sons, the citizens and those who wear the uniform. The fallen will forever be engraved in the history of our nation's heroism. Their sacrifice, their courage, their love of life, and their dedication to the ideals we hold dear are a testament to the power that resides in our hearts.

We must not and cannot forget, not even for a moment, all of our abducted people. It is hard to imagine a more complex and excruciating journey than the journey of the families whose loved ones are at the hands of Hamas murderers. We all carry a prayer that the

241

words of the prophet will be fulfilled in us, "And our children return to their own borders."

We will also mourn the loss of youthful joy, the coveted heroism, the holiness of the will and the devotion of the soul who perished in the heavy battle. We will weep for the lives of many, too many who were robbed by a cruel hand victim of monstrous and unbridled anti-Semitic violence. And yet we remember that even in the darkest hours, we witnessed the greatness of the soul, the bravery, resilience, and compassion that built us as a people. The infinite Israeli spirit that refuses to be broken.

Indeed, we made a grave and painful mistake when we were not ready. Still, the most terrible mistake was that of the enemy, the enemy whose "great heroes" murdered, massacred, raped, and butchered toddlers, the elderly, girls, and boys, burned down houses with living humans inside and committed the worst crimes against humanity. This enemy brought destruction and disaster to his cities and his people. An enemy who displays the book "Mein Kampf" by Hitler proudly in the rooms of his house and whose summer camps were camps of murderous brainwashing and blind hatred. An enemy who thought he knew us and underestimated the bravery of our sons and daughters until he saw with his own eyes how "a people that rises like a lion leaps up like a lion."

The heroic forces of our people astonishingly erupted from him. We have seen the "TikTok generation," which is "a generation of ancient times, a brave, strong, time-honored people "whose heroism will be engraved in the history of Israel.

I have met with the fighters and commanders who led the forces cast from steel, striving for contact and swearing, "No More!"

I saw the strength of the evacuated communities and families, the bravery of our wounded in the hospitals, the faith and burning pride of the grieving families, the volunteerism and solidarity in Israeli society, Arabs and Jews alike, and the determination of our allies who stand by us led by the United States, the Diaspora Jewry that stands with us as one with one heart, sometimes at self-risk. There is no shadow of a doubt in my heart: no one can defeat a nation with such sons and daughters; No one will be able to divide our close-knit and united people.

Although the war broke out in one of the most polarized periods in our history, and while the enemy hoped that the terrorist attack would deepen the rifts and weaken the Israeli alliance, we chose life. We decided to unite immediately and fight shoulder-to-shoulder for the present and future of our typical home.

Unfortunately, it is hard not to see that some choose at this time to return to the discourse of hate that prevailed here until October 6th. Any withdrawal to those polarization regions directly threatens our safety and lives. You are always allowed to criticize, and sometimes you have to argue it is part of our DNA, but it is time to show responsibility, keep our togetherness, and remember that we are one nation and one country. Hamas must not be allowed to win the battle for Israeli unity. This is true for all of us and undoubtedly true for elected officials and the leadership. Leadership during war means responsibility for Israeli cohesion, the basis of victory. As our brothers and sisters risk their lives on the front lines, we must rise above the campaigns, above the petty politics and the divisive and toxic discourse both about the day before and about the day after - and listen to the cry of our children who demand, "Instead of blessing us to come home in peace, let us come home in peace. Peace is within us."

Despite the challenges we face, I do not doubt that we will emerge from the shadow of the campaign more robust and more determined than ever. Together, as one nation, we will overcome the darkness, rise from the ashes, build, plant and sow, affix the mezuzahs[1], turn every hell into heaven, and create a future of hope and prosperity for our people, our country and the entire region one that will be worthy of the sacrifice of the fallen, will lift the spirits of the victims, and will reflect our commitment to place a beacon of hope, for us and all of humanity.

Our enemy was wrong. The spirit of the people of Israel always won. Our spirit will win this time, too.

January 14th, 2024

---

1. A parchment scroll, on which the 'Shema' is handwritten by an expert scribe, is mounted on the right side of the doorpost of a Jewish home. It reminds us of God and our heritage and invites God's watchful care over the home.

Made in the USA
Las Vegas, NV
14 October 2024

3902b6f7-c793-4b7b-9080-8ef6117211d7R01